IN THE SHADOW OF THE ROCKS

IN THE SHADOW OF THE ROCKS

Archaeology of the Chimney Rock District
in Southern Colorado

FLORENCE C. LISTER

UNIVERSITY PRESS OF COLORADO

Copyright © 1993 by the University Press of Colorado
Published by the University Press of Colorado
P.O. Box 849
Niwot, Colorado 80544

The University Press of Colorado is a cooperative publishing enterprise supported, in part, by Adams State College, Colorado State University, Fort Lewis College, Mesa State College, Metropolitan State College of Denver, University of Colorado, University of Northern Colorado, University of Southern Colorado, and Western State College of Colorado.

Produced in cooperation with
San Juan National Forest Association and the Amoco Foundation.

Cover photo by Jim Fuge.

Library of Congress Cataloging-in-Publication Data

Lister, Florence Cline.
    In the shadow of the rocks: archaeology of the Chimney Rock District in southern Colorado / Florence C. Lister.
      p. cm.
    Includes bibliographical references and index.
    ISBN 0-87081-292-0 (acid-free paper)
    1. Pueblo Indians — Antiquities. 2. Indians of North America —Colorado — Chimney Rock Region (Archuleta County) — Antiquities. 3. Chimney Rock Region (Archuleta County, Colo.) — Antiquities. 4. Colorado — Antiquities.
I. Title.
E99.P9L518 1993
978.8'32 — dc20   93-13293
                                                             CIP

The paper used in this publication meets the minimum requirements of the American National Standard for Information Sciences — Permanence of Paper for Printed Library Materials. ANSI Z39.48–1984

∞

10 9 8 7 6 5 4 3 2 1

CONTENTS

FIGURES

PREFACE

In 1970, 3,160 acres of the Pagosa district of the San Juan National Forest were set aside as the Chimney Rock Archeological Area, making it the largest high-mountain archaeological zone in the national forest system. It is situated within the boundaries of the Southern Ute Indian Reservation and is a special precinct to these Native Americans. Also in 1970, a 960-acre block of land containing the greatest concentration of prehistoric remains in the national forest system was placed on the National Register of Historic Places. Subsequently, an intensive National Park Service/University of New Mexico research project in Chaco Canyon National Monument underscored the connection of the major Chimney Rock site to a pan–San Juan Basin Chacoan system, and legislation was put before Congress to add the Chimney Rock Archeological Area to the Chaco Archeological Protection Site System. These various designations are part of long-term programs to protect the antiquities and make them available to the public through development of visitor facilities and understandable through interpretive materials.

The southern base of the pinnacles of Companion and Chimney rocks has the added value of being an aerie of peregrine falcons. These birds of prey typically nest at the top of high talus slopes having ledges with gravel or soil into which depressions for eggs can be scraped. The protection of this endangered species and its habitat is a second mission incorporated into the area's management.

This publication necessarily goes beyond the territory immediately surrounding Chimney Rock in order to establish the cultural background from which the local expression evolved and to carry interpretation through to modern historic occupations. Two thousand years of human history are represented. I needed the aid of many people in presenting this long continuum. Thanks are extended to Curtis Schaafsma, Louise Stiver, Rosemary Talley, and Willow Powers, Museum of

New Mexico; Helen Pustmeuller, Department of Anthropology, University of Denver; Katherine Kane, Anne Bond, and Mary Sullivan, Colorado Historical Society; Robert McDaniel, Animas Valley Museum; Nancy Hammack, Complete Archaeological Service Associates; Charles H. Lange, formerly University of Northern Illinois; Gary Matlock and Tom McMurray, San Juan National Forest; Laurie Gruel, San Juan National Forest Association; John W. Sanders and Bob Snyder, San Juan Basin Archaeological Society. Some specimen photographs were taken by Gary G. Lister. Funding by the Amoco Foundation is gratefully acknowledged.

Most important to the temporal and cultural framework of this summary were the thorough technical reports on both the Navajo Reservoir and Chimney Rock areas by Frank W. Eddy, University of Colorado. In general, the reconstructions of the past presented here are his. However, in the years since Eddy's work, varying interpretations have been put forth, and they are included where germane. Thanks are also due Eddy for generous permission to use an assortment of unpublished field photographs.

This book should have been my husband's to write. On behalf of the University of Colorado, he negotiated the original agreements with the Southern Ute Indian Tribe and the San Juan National Forest to conduct archaeological surveys and excavations on their lands. When the San Juan National Forest Association and the San Juan Basin Archaeological Society decided to sponsor a synthesis for the interested public of the prehistoric human drama played out in the upper San Juan district, he agreed to do the job. But that was not to be.

Therefore, with the guidance of four valued family friends and distinguished regional archaeologists — David A. Breternitz, W. James Judge, Marcia Truell Newren, and R. Gwinn Vivian — I have endeavored to fulfill this commitment. With such expertise at hand, any shortcomings in the text obviously are my sole responsibility.

So this book is for you, Robert H. Lister (1915–1990): educator, digger, administrator, lecturer, father, and my love.

FLORENCE C. LISTER
Mancos, Colorado

PART I
THE PLACE

1

LA PIEDRA PARADA

Two stone pinnacles loom side by side on an elevated promontory overlooking the head of the Piedra River valley in south central Colorado. They scratch the hard blue sky for rain and snow, often are obscured by swirling cloud banks, and at times seem to stand defiant before brilliant bolts of summer lightning that rip the firmament. Behind them tower the San Juan Mountains, evergreen on lower slopes, bald and formidable above, and comprising an arm of the massif that diverts continental waters east and west. At their feet to the south sweeps a variegated panorama of broken ramparts and tablelands stiffly folding down to the semidesert lands embracing an interior basin, through which slices the San Juan River, major tributary to the upper Colorado River. At a distance the small Piedra, the easternmost substantial stream of the secondary network, meanders in quiet counterpoint through a shallow U-shaped depression and bordering floodplains on its way from the snowmelt of the Rockies to its merger with the San Juan. Their former confluence now is blocked by the impounded waters of the man-made Navajo Reservoir. The view to the west is obstructed by tiers of cliffs and high blue mesas that level down to the Pine River valley. To the east rises a barricade of successive ranges, each reaching greater heights and structural complexity. Here, where the two stony pinnacles eternally stand guard, the expansive plateau of the northern Southwest finally is boxed in.

Eighteenth-century Spaniards called the spires *La Piedra Parada*, the upright or standing rock. Less eloquently, nineteenth-century Americans referred to them as Chimney Rock, one of many natural monuments in the West with the identical name. Strangely, both terms were

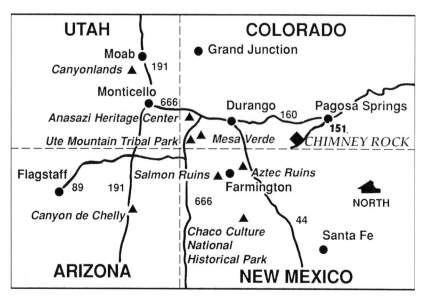

Regional map of upper San Juan district showing location of the Chimney Rock Archeological Area.

used in the singular, which may reflect the fact that just one of the pillars is immediately apparent when seen straight on from east or west. Lower in height, greater in mass, and with less pleasing contours, the westerly one remained anonymous until an archaeologist alluded to it in the 1920s as the companion to the more spectacular adjacent Chimney Rock. Henceforth, the unnamed tower had an identity: Companion Rock.

Although the various Native American names for these stelae of nature are not known, assuredly the columns were recognized by the aborigines as landmarks having possible mythological significance. Modern Pueblo Indians generally consider such unique physiographic features to be representations of certain deities or spirits. If their predecessors had similar animistic beliefs, the rare pair of dominant shafts of stone rising more than a thousand feet above the nearby valley floor may have been regarded as the earthly symbols of the Twin War Gods, now prominent figures in the religious pantheon of the Pueblos. Believers regard them as offspring of the Sun God, born at the time of creation;

in some versions of the legendary accounts they built mountains and in others merely lived there. One of their attributes is the ability to turn themselves or their antagonists into stone. As prominent mountains and natural stone columns are both present in this locale, the attribution seems reasonable. However, if Chimney Rock and its companion were indeed viewed as sacred embodiments of the Twin War Gods, the prehistoric shrine we would expect to find in a cairn of rocks at their base with offerings of miniature bows and arrows, war clubs, shields, or prayer plumes placed on it has been stolen by time.

In geological terms, Chimney and Companion rocks are dramatic survivors of an inexorable process of erosion that for eons has been wearing down the Colorado Plateau and carrying it grain by grain to western waters. The two spires are unstable remnants of a relatively modest layer of tawny bedded rock, now called Pictured Cliff sandstone, that was deposited beneath an ancient inland sea. Blocky chunks of the chimneys themselves continue to break away and cascade down steep talus slopes formed by a soft, thick accumulation of dark Cretaceous shale. Plant matter and small organisms that fell into the coalescing sandstone stratum became fossilized and today, millions of years later, weather out of the matrix. Reported fossil patterns of ferns and sea shells confirm the passage of an earlier, warmer, watery episode. The geologic movement that crunched the mountain mass upward to the north simultaneously tilted the blocky landform on which the sandstone steeples would slowly be left freestanding. The rest of its more-or-less flat top sloped about ten degrees from northeast to southwest, with convoluted long inclines fanning down to the east and south and a precipitous escarpment exposed on the north face. In the Southwest the Spanish term *cuesta* is used to define such a formation, which in this instance appears as a final bridging platform between the lower San Juan Basin to the south and the lofty Rocky Mountains to the north. Water-ways encircle the base of the cuesta at about 6,400 feet above sea level, whereas the cuesta surface reaches 7,600 feet, culminating in the Chimney Rock at an additional 300 feet. Along the north side an intermittent stream, Devil Creek, flows though a narrow defile separating the Chimney Rock mesa from the San Juan foothills and empties into the perennial Piedra River on the west. During the Pleistocene period, as the Piedra ate deeper into its channel, stepped terraces were left above it at the western end of the lower Chimney Rock mesa. To the east and south of the cuesta, another small Piedra tributary, Stollsteimer Creek, sluggishly moves southwest in years of sufficient moisture through a valley more expansive and open than that of Devil Creek.

The vegetational cover of the Piedra River district reflects increased elevation and precipitation as one moves the twenty miles upstream from the San Juan to the headgates formed by the Chimney Rock cuesta on the east and Petersen Mesa on the west, above which open space for horticulture is choked off. A riparian environment of willows, cotton-woods, rushes, and grasses marks the riverine bottom lands. Gravel-paved embankments lead up to sage- and brush-covered silt benches. Occasional stands of scrub oak, piñon, and juniper become thicker near the jagged mountain wall. A reversal of the usual life-zone pattern occurs at the towering Chimney Rock mesa: here, a relic yellow pine forest grows on lower southeastern slopes, while piñon and juniper trees stand on higher ground. This role-reversal is due to the cold winter air that drains into the narrow valleys. Steep clay ridges capped with sandstone and rocky cliff faces make up some of the exposed surfaces. However, before the introduction of sheep a hundred years ago, the area upriver was notable for billowing carpets of waist-high grasses and exuberantly blooming wildflowers that served to accentuate the valley's transitional linkage between the extremes of the denuded southern basin, where trees and other greenery are a novelty, and the aspen- and pine-forested northern mountains and lush but soggy alpine meadows.

Unpredictability characterized the regional climate. In modern times annual precipitation has averaged a little less than eighteen inches. Much of it comes with a vengeance. Often developing and then departing in the space of a few hours, violent summer thunderstorms boil the rivers with a supercharge of sediments as normally dry channels are flushed out bank to bank. Such rapid runoff reduces the amount of beneficial moisture reaching plant roots. At the opposite end of the spectrum are cyclical droughts, some lasting season after season. In winter, snows typically drift many feet deep. Accumulations on shaded slopes linger for months. At these times subzero temperatures are the norm. There are generally only three or four months a year when freezing

4

does not occur. At best the average overall monthly temperature is in the forty-to-fifty degree range. But just as every July or August does not experience rain, not every January or February is completely snowbound.

Despite their picture-postcard beauty, these uplands of the Chimney Rock district, the northernmost outpost of the vast Colorado Plateau, have not sustained prosperous human occupation. The reasons range from topographic inhospitability to ecological stresses to historical circumstances. For the past millennium they have tested the mettle of a veritable parade of diverse cultures. But in the end they essentially remain, as they were in the beginning, the legendary province of the Twin War Gods.

PART II
THE ARCHAEOLOGY

2

THE DIGGERS ARRIVE

From the time of the first Spanish *entradas* in the last quarter of the eighteenth century, the upper San Juan Basin was known to contain scores of small ruins of unknown age and affiliation. It was not until the post–Civil War era, however, that they came to the attention of the public. Spanish-Americans out of New Mexico and Anglos from east of the Rockies began to traverse or settle the Chimney Rock district, noting numerous remains seemingly unrelated to the modern Utes then roaming the mesas and valleys. On an 1878 road survey trip into the San Juan Mountains, Lt. C.A.H. McCauley reported, "Long before the advent of the White man upon the continent [the San Juan River's] banks teemed with an unknown population of whose habits and mode of life history speaks. Only tradition is silent, with naught to aid the intelligent investigator save fragmentary pottery and the ruins of their dwellings" (Motter 1984, 45). Settlers clearing land for construction and gardens saw low knolls of stones, some encircling bowl-shaped depressions, that appeared to be collapsed houses. Bits of broken pottery, arrowheads, and stone flakes left from tool manufacture were strewn about. When the mounds were considered detrimental to farm development, they were leveled. A limited amount of leisure-time digging in the sites took place in order to secure "relics," particularly pottery vessels. However, the pottery and the sites themselves were so unprepossessing that the ruins generally were viewed merely as local curiosities. That fact, plus the very limited population moving into the Piedra Valley, helped to keep the bulk of the ruins from being vandalized.

According to an account in the *Pagosa Springs Sun* (February 28, 1930), one log house on a piece of land at the junction of Yellowjacket and Squaw creeks three miles west of the Piedra Valley was "foundationed on the unfortunate ruins of the Aztecs." This article reflected a widespread belief in the late nineteenth century among farmers and ranchers that these evidences of an earlier occupation had been left behind by the Aztec Indians. That opinion originated in a popular book, *The History of the Conquest of Mexico* by William H. Prescott, which recounted an Aztec legend stating that their ancestors arrived in central Mexico after lengthy peregrinations from the far north. Without the benefit of archaeological research to prove otherwise, the association of the San Juan antiquities with the Mexican migrations was logical. (More scientific minds linked the vestiges of the past with the present-day Pueblo Indians.) However, the Aztecs did not emerge as an identifiable entity until several centuries after the upper San Juan area had been abandoned by its prehistoric occupants. The north from which the Aztecs came now is believed to have been the north central tableland of Mexico. In other words, the Aztecs were never on the San Juan, nor did they ever see the pair of dominant natural stone columns at the head of the Piedra drainage.

No scientific work was undertaken in the Piedra Valley until 1921. In that year J. A. Jeancon left the Smithsonian Institution to become curator of archaeology and ethnology at the State Historical and Natural History Society in Denver. He hit the ground running. With an avowed goal of getting Colorado involved in its own archaeology, in April he was off on an inspection trip to the southern part of the state, near Pagosa Springs. Based on photographs and observations of local parties, he believed there were many prehistoric sites in the vicinity.

At the beginning of the twenties, the growing ranks of Southwestern prehistorians had only sketchy ideas about the aboriginal societies that had developed on the Colorado Plateau and then inexplicably disappeared. Generally speaking, the large wrecked structures in open country and those hunkered down in alcoves in cliff faces had been the first to be studied because of their visibility, often spectacular settings, and the lure of large amounts of material goods found to be within them. The State Historical and Natural History Society had in its possession one of the collections the Wetherill brothers took from the Mesa Verde cliff dwellings in the 1890s. Stimulated by these finds, Richard Wetherill went on to participate in a four-year excavation at the huge bottomland settlement of Pueblo Bonito in Chaco Canyon. He and others of his time correctly thought that both the cliff dwellings and the ruins at Chaco represented a prehistoric climax to a long, entangled growth process that culminated in the modern Pueblo Indians of the Rio Grande, Zuni, and Hopi areas.

Between these two projects dealing with the supposedly final developmental stage on the Colorado Plateau, the Wetherills uncovered a manifestation of a different order. On the basis of the lack of architecture (other than storage cists scooped out of soft dirt alcove floors in escarpments of southeastern Utah) and primitive material arts (other than basketry taken from the alcove deposits), the diggers postulated that what they found represented an initial cultural evolutionary phase occurring centuries earlier than that of the cliff dwellings and perhaps involving a different aboriginal stock. The latter notion stemmed from a variant shape to skulls removed from burial sites. Richard Wetherill named this group of people the Basketmakers. Between these speculated earliest and latest expressions of aboriginal life on the Colorado Plateau, there remained a gaping void of perhaps many centuries.

At the exact time Jeancon took on his new job, a five-year excavation effort at a massive site at Aztec, New Mexico, sponsored by the prestigious American Museum of Natural History, was concluding amid a great deal of national press. That settlement on the Animas River just below the Colorado border obviously was erected by masons familiar with techniques used at Pueblo Bonito and was inhabited during the time the regional culture came to full flower. But elsewhere across southern Colorado and northern New Mexico, there were less pretentious remains of potential significance in filling the data gap between the beginning and end of the postulated prehistoric chronology. Jeancon made no bones about his desire to get himself and his new home institution in on the action.

An amateur archaeologist who was familiar with regional sites and had participated in some of the excavations at Aztec Ruins, J. S. Palmer, guided Jeancon to a locality that was densely occupied prehistorically. That was the Chimney Rock cuesta. As the men reached the upper slopes of the mesa, they met a series of craterlike pits, obviously man-made, rounded by massive stones held in place by mud mortar. These pits crowded one after another up the steep edges of the mesa. As the explorers ascended a ridge no more than twelve feet wide pointing toward the base of the pinnacles, they crossed what appeared to be portions of one small room that lay directly in their trail. Higher up, where the mesa flattened out again, stood an impressive mound covered with the debris of fallen masonry and low scrub growth. The men did not doubt that it once was a substantial dwelling, perhaps of many rooms and several stories, isolated at the highest spot on the mesa where occupation could possibly have occurred. The ruin was separated from the foot of Companion Rock by a twenty-foot-deep saddle in the sandstone surface of the mesa, above which soared the column. The collapsed structure promised productive exploration. Its siting on a barren rock platform hundreds of yards up from the nearest source of water was puzzling, but the view in all directions was breathtaking.

When Jeancon and Palmer returned, they called upon several ranchers working land on the Piedra terraces at the cuesta's western toe. One of these was a member of the Pargin family, who had come across the plains from Missouri after the Civil War and settled on the Piedra about 1902. He and his neighbors showed their visitors other sites that, although overgrown with sage, appeared to differ from those on the Chimney Rock mesa. A possible temporal distinction was implied. If verified, it would give archaeologists an opportunity to study a progression through time of regional culture.

Exhilarated by what he saw, Jeancon set about immediately to ready a field expedition. First, through the efforts of E. B. Renaud, professor of Romance languages, he secured the collaboration of the University of Denver. This institution aided in soliciting funds and provided five student field hands. One of these was Frank H. H. Roberts, Jr., later to become a stalwart in the formative period of Southwestern archaeology. Next, Jeancon worked through U.S. Senator L. C. Phipps of Colorado and Jesse Walter Fewkes, his former boss and head of the Bureau of American Ethnology at the Smithsonian Institution, to obtain an excavation permit from the U.S. Department of Agriculture. This agency had jurisdiction over the Chimney Rock environs because they were within a national forest. The Colorado highway department loaned the expedition a two-ton truck to haul necessary gear to the field and bring specimens back to Denver.

The Chimney Rock expedition was launched that June. In 1921 the roads away from the more settled areas along the east face of the Rockies were little more than wagon traces. The one over Wolf Creek Pass had been completed just five years earlier and was meant for automobiles. It was a dirt roadbed twelve feet wide with few places where vehicles going in opposite directions could pass. In some spots rocky outcrops project-ing from the cliffs required soft car tops to be lowered. On the opposite side of the road were sheer drops of many hundreds of feet. The party needed two days to grind up the steep switchbacks. From Pagosa Springs on the south side to Chimney Rock, the road was worse. In wet weather it often took as many as fifty-two hours to go the twenty-two miles from town to the cuesta. That June was dry, however, and in a matter of half a day the excavators were on location. They pitched camp on a bench above Devil Creek at the northwest end of the mesa, where four men from the San Juan area, including Palmer, joined the ranks. The follow-ing three days were spent clearing an abandoned logging road so that all vehicles could reach the camp and building a mile-long footpath up the mesa to the archaeological sites on top.

Excavation began at the head of the trail with the opening of two circular-to-rectangular single-room structures, with some rough stone walls still standing up to seven feet in height. The rooms appeared to have served domestic functions because milling bins, stone grinding implements, fragments of pottery, a stone axe, one bone awl, and charred corn were found in them, along with hearths and a sandstone bench next to one wall. The floors were smoothed by a layer of adobe mud spread over the irregular caprock of the mesa. Each unit was roofed originally with an undetermined pattern of wooden poles covered with branches, earth, and sandstone slabs. Slab paving was noticed outside the rooms.

According to Jeancon's count, the vaguely round depressions indi-cating shelters on the mesa top numbered 107. Some were no more than ten feet in diameter; others were over forty feet across. Most had been placed along the east, west, and north edges of the prominence, the south part of the landform being unsuitable for architectural purposes because

The 1921 field camp of the State Historical and Natural History Society at the north base of the Chimney Rock pinnacles. *Courtesy University of Denver.*

of deep canyons slicing back into it. None of these stone-lined hollows was cleared of its overburden that season, though, because all hands were eager to get to work on the centerpiece mound high up in the shadow of the rocks.

A narrow ridge separating the lower and upper levels of the mesa top, with sheer slopes on either side and an incline projecting upward for seventy-five feet, struck Jeancon as a natural defense. He called it "the causeway." At its summit the party undertook to excavate the low walls of block masonry remaining from a circular room set within an oblong terrace. The room was elaborated with a small antechamber, a firepit, and a depressed pot rest. To judge from a modest assortment of artifacts taken from its fill, the usage was secular. Nevertheless, because of its strategic position blocking access to the upper mesa, on which the principal structure sat, Jeancon referred to the ruin as "the guardhouse."

The large pueblo on the uppermost, triangular mesa level proved to be a well-built, compact, L-shaped unit over two hundred feet long on its southern side. It was divided into an estimated thirty-five ground-level rooms, some commodious, others small. These wrapped around two circular ceremonial rooms, or kivas. The amount and type of debris in places confirmed a partial second story along the north side that had fallen. Some of the walls, of an estimated twenty on the upper level, were still standing up to fourteen feet in height. Their profiles were plumb, and their corners were squared but not bonded. They were constructed with an outer veneer surface of coursed thick and thin sandstone blocks broken from the matrix rock upon which the building was placed, over an inner core of stones and mud. Originally, wall surfaces were probably mud plastered; because of exposure and moisture, all such fragile coating was gone. Jeancon determined through careful inspection of all junctures that an exterior shell of the structure was put in place first, interior partitions being added subsequently. This studied approach implied a master plan, not a haphazard adding-on as the need arose. Since the pueblo stood on bare rock, floors had to be leveled by filling in uneven surfaces with mud. The entire floor then was thickly frosted with liquid adobe that hardened. A sufficient number of roof elements was found to hypothesize about its design: a pattern of primary and secondary beams topped with brush and a copious earthen layer.

Work of the 1921 season completely or partially cleared five of what were regarded primarily as dwellings, all notable for their large size (more than twenty feet in length). Two of these rooms produced such a noteworthy find of manos (grinding stones), metates (larger grinding slabs), and potsherds that they were believed to have been storage facilities. Additionally, ten small rectangular units surrounding the eastern kiva were emptied. These may have been used for storage; more likely they were filled with dirt and some crossbars to serve as reinforcing cellular buttresses to counter the outward thrust of the large kiva. They probably were roofed at the same level as the adjacent kiva to create a broad public space in front of the two-story roomblock to the north. Other work areas were at a premium because of the constriction of the mesa.

The eastern kiva was set down within a rectangular enclosure whose wall height matched that of the kiva. Given the placement of the village on bedrock, the kiva could not be sunk into the ground, and so the

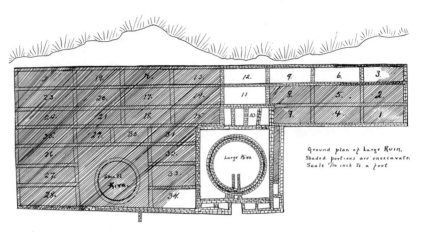

Jeancon's 1921 drawing of the ground plan of the Chimney Rock pueblo showing excavated rooms. *After Jeancon, 1922, Plate XII.*

subterranean effect had to be simulated by this means. Jeancon marveled that, without engineering equipment, the builders had erected a true circle. Walls were of fine coursed masonry, in one area still coated with mud plaster. A low bench encircled the base of the chamber, with horizontal beam rests spaced on top of it. Diggers encountered two floor levels resulting from remodeling. A pair of short horizontal tunnels, superimposed one above the other, projected into the chamber and connected at the other end into a single vertical shaft in the south wall. These provided necessary ventilation — there were no other openings to the chamber except a probable hatchway in the roof. The crew did not find a ceremonial floor opening to the spirit world, or *sipapu*, in either floor. They did find a hearth, but because it was not directly in line with the ventilator tunnel mouth, the vertical stone slab normally placed to prevent currents from blowing ash or smoke into the room was absent.

As for roof construction, the evidence suggested that four spaced upright posts had supported a square central frame, to which were attached horizontal beams penetrating the kiva walls, stabilized by short uprights secured in the bench-top beam rests. Over this basic roof skeleton lay a herringbone arrangement of small secondary timbers

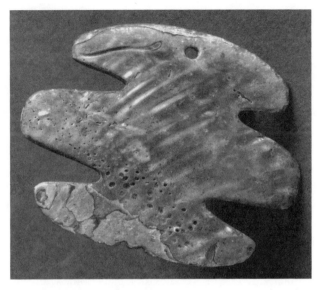

Unusual trilobed abalone shell pendant or gorget recovered in the upper ventilator shaft of the east kiva of the Chimney Rock pueblo. The material must have been imported along lengthy trade channels from the Pacific Coast, but manufacture could have taken place anywhere en route, if not locally. *Courtesy Colorado Historical Society.*

covered with brush, earth, and an outer paving of unmortared sandstone slabs.

At the end of the season's exploration, Jeancon was convinced that the Chimney Rock pueblo, although distinct from its immediate neighbors, represented a local effort. He regarded the workmanship as excellent, the effort required to quarry stone in situ and to transport earth and water to the locale as staggering. Notwithstanding what he called "indigenous accomplishments," he also suspected an undefined relationship in the style of the Chimney Rock pueblo with that of Pueblo Bonito, the largest settlement in Chaco Canyon some ninety miles to the south (then being studied by a team sponsored by the National Geographic Society) and with that at Aztec Ruins, about forty miles to the southwest, where excavations had just halted.

Between the Chimney Rock pueblo and the place where the sandstone crust of the mesa drops sharply before rising into the bedding of

Companion Rock, the State Historical and Natural History Society crew observed a sizable depression where at one time raging fires had permanently reddened the stone. What happened there? Was rubbish burned? Unlikely. Both ancient and modern Pueblo Indians typically disposed of trash over the nearest cliff, in a heap in a nearby designated spot, in abandoned house rooms, or all around the outskirts. Were the fires ceremonial? Perhaps. The siting of the village in such difficult, awesome surroundings suggests a ritualistic intent. Did the Twin War Gods look down upon special rites? Was cremation of the dead one of them? Were the dead prisoners or protectors? Just below the adjacent northern rimrock, the field party discovered a two-hundred-foot-long strip of the sloughing mesa sides where a solidified mass of calcined human bones, pottery fragments, and other artifacts had accumulated. The diggers thought they detected clearings for pyres there. However, it is possible that the actual incineration of bodies took place somewhere else. Above, in the pit in naked rock? The improbable setting of the pueblo likewise could have been chosen with an eye to defense. If so, maybe the fires ignited on the Chimney Rock promontory served as signals to a network of allies? The plot to this story of the ancients of Chimney Rock decidedly thickened.

Down at the west base of the cuesta, preliminary observations confirmed the ranchers' reports of ruins, but the institution's team was astounded at their number. The men reconnoitered the first and second terraces south along both sides of the Piedra River, counting them by the dozens. However, compared to the Chimney Rock pueblo, these sites did not amount to much. They stood out as either small, low hillocks or circular pits blanketed with sage, generally the first plant to revegetate disturbed ground in the Southwest. Jagged chunks of burned adobe, some with beam impressions, and a few potsherds covered the surfaces. Some sites were strung out in a line along the bench tops. Others were clustered close together, on occasion rimming a depression of considerable circumference. Jeancon theorized that this particular settlement pattern represented single-family dwellings surrounding some sort of communal gathering place.

As they turned to the riverine remains, the student diggers found the going tougher and less exciting than at the Chimney Rock pueblo.

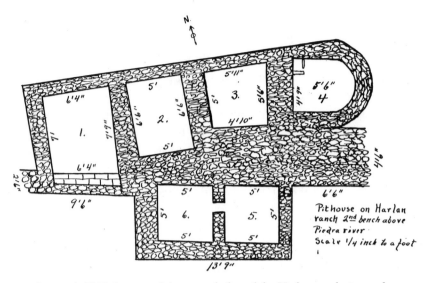

Jeancon's 1921 drawing of the ground plan of the Harlan ranch site at the western base of the Chimney Rock cuesta. *After Jeancon, 1922, Plate VI.*

The difficulty was due to the amorphous, ill-defined nature of the structures involved. Walls often were hard to trace, and shapes of rooms were unpredictable. The students found some one-room dwellings sunk a foot or more into the soil, with upper walls of rounded river cobbles slumped into great piles of mud and rock. Although Jeancon termed these structures "pithouses," later research elsewhere in the San Juan Basin restricted that definition to shelters of much greater depth wherein the surrounding earth formed walls and provided insulation. One mound covered what had been a complex of very small contiguous surface rooms made of variable combinations of adobe, cobblestone, and horizontally laid sandstone slabs. In some instances the walls still bore coats of mud plaster. The lack of connecting doorways suggested entrance through flat roofs made of poles, brush, and earth. Some floors were paved with pieces of sandstone glued into place with adobe mud, which, as any Southwesterner knows, is the stickiest of substances.

One unusual structure excavated in this first season was an isolated circular building approximately fifteen feet in diameter having very thick cobblestone walls that originally rose to an estimated height of ten feet. An interior hearth and an assortment of artifacts pointed to domestic occupation. Even so, Jeancon called this unit a tower, implying that he thought it something other than an ordinary family residence. To him, it was part of a defense system that probably incorporated many other comparable structures in the vicinity. By the end of the next season, he had decided that the sixty-five to seventy-five round structures of the mesa were indeed military towers. Towers also had been identified in the Mesa Verde province to the west of Chimney Rock and south on the Jemez Plateau of New Mexico. Whether they were erected to serve as lookout posts had not been determined.

Restricted digging in 1921 convinced Jeancon that further research would reveal at least six stages in the local prehistoric architectural development. His theorized chronology began with one-room dwellings partially set down into the ground and advanced to the above-ground multiroomed complex of carefully crafted sandstone masonry blocks. According to information at the time, Basketmaker culture was not represented in the former, but classic Pueblo was in the latter. Perhaps Jeancon did have evidence to fill the gap in between. He had no idea how long such an evolutionary process might have taken, nor did he entertain the possibility of contemporaneity. In that early period of researching the area's prehistory, a simplistic progression from crude to complex architecture was assumed and thought to have encompassed three or four thousand years.

Further substantiation of a cultural developmental sequence from early to late came through recovered pottery. Fragments from the so-called pithouses were coarse; Jeancon believed they were punched from a wad of clay rather than created by a coiling method. These fragments primarily were tiny, gray, and rough-surfaced, and the vessels presumably were used for storage or for cooking over open fires. Many pieces were warped out of shape because of the potter's carelessness or lack of skill. A few were decorated with crudely executed black designs on an untreated gray surface. Later forms were what Jeancon called heart-shaped jars with round bodies closing in to very small mouths, dippers made from a small bowl attached to a troughed handle that in cross-section duplicated a gourd sliced in half, and wide-mouthed, bag-shaped jars.

Unfired balls of clay, shaped by being thrust while moist into orifices of earthenware containers, also were recovered.

The pottery from the commanding pueblo beneath the stone columns was of better quality and, Jeancon believed, of a later time. Vessel size had increased. The number of shapes had expanded to include bladder-shaped jars, handled pitchers, and bowls. Utility types from that site retained the bag-shaped, tapered-bottom forms, but some had purposefully textured exteriors, with construction coils crimped successively as they were added upward in the pot's formation. However, a frequent diagonal patterning to the impressions made it appear as if the pots had been twisted in a screw. The interiors of these vessels were smoothed so as not to catch food particles. For some unknown reason, Jeancon referred to these as "flower pots." That was an unfortunate choice of words — the round-bottomed vessels could not have stood erect without yucca fiber rings or supporting depressions in earth, and there was no clue that the ancients raised flowers. He also unaccountably compared the pots to flat-bottomed, often highly decorated Chaco cylindrical vessels, which some modern students consider to be a specialized ceramic introduction from Mexico restricted to ceremonial use. Most Chimney Rock pueblo service vessels were enhanced with a set of simple black geometric patterns painted over a white slip that afforded greater contrast between ground and design and masked imperfections in the base material. Draftsmanship and format layout were improved over earlier pottery-making efforts. Again, Jeancon felt that some influence from the Chaco region was apparent in specific design motifs. He also was reminded of pottery from the Gallina area of northern New Mexico, where he had worked prior to his move to Colorado. Still, Jeancon asserted that Chimney Rock pottery remained distinctive enough to be recognizable. A fair number of fragments were red in color, and Jeancon at first considered these to have been parts of containers traded into the Chimney Rock district. Later he concluded that poorer specimens likely were native, an opinion subsequent theorists would reject.

Now and then the excavators exhumed human remains during the course of their investigations and took note of what they thought might be extensive burial reserves along the river benches. Some bones were so fragile that they crumbled upon being touched. Others were so well preserved that burial position and sex of the individual could be determined. Associated pottery offerings were occasionally collected. Jeancon interpreted the finds of calcined bone fragments, some strewn in beds of charcoal and ash, as evidence for the practice of cremation.

The State Historical and Natural History Society's work in the 1921 season aroused the curiosity of numerous people living in the Chimney Rock area, who long had felt their place had importance to other folks in other times. Jeancon said he showed more than five hundred of them through the digs. Considering the ruins' isolation and the difficulty of getting to them, he may have exaggerated that number to impress his board of directors.

On his return to Denver, Jeancon continued lobbying the board for what had become his pet project. Excitedly he reported to the members in a 1924 manuscript, "The Pagosa field is so far beyond the expectations, in extent, interest and accessibility, that your curator begs you to exert every means at your disposal to continue the work in that field. Here is the opportunity to do big things and Colorado has never had a bigger chance to place herself in the limelight as at this time." He assured the board that Alfred V. Kidder, then the most highly regarded scientist in the discipline, had stated that exploration of Archuleta County, incorporating the Chimney Rock–Piedra district, was the most important archaeological study then underway in the entire United States. This claim was also an overstatement, but it helped the board persuade the state legislature to appropriate $4,500 for another period of field work.

There were snags. A $700,000 shortfall was discovered in the state budget for 1922, and the researchers had to undertake a fund-raising drive. Enough public-spirited citizens responded with contributions that, with a complementary grant from the University of Denver, a total larger than that originally budgeted by the state was eventually amassed.

While the financing was in doubt, Jeancon fretted that someone else would usurp rights in what he then thought of as his personal research domain. Palmer, for one, had applied for an excavation permit to dig in the Chimney Rock area. Jeancon urgently contacted his friend Fewkes and was successful in getting the application denied on the grounds that Palmer was not academically trained or institutionally connected.

Meanwhile, the State Historical and Natural History Society was granted its own two-year permit, with the proviso that work commence within thirty days. With no money in hand, it seemed unlikely that the condition could be met. Jeancon protested to all who would listen that out-of-staters were robbing Colorado of its patrimony. It was a fact that much of the regional archaeology of the time was carried on by persons from Eastern institutions; up until the previous year Jeancon himself had been among them. Jeancon furthered his argument by noting that foreign governments were also benefiting from the state's antiquities, a reference to a collection of Mesa Verde artifacts sent to Sweden thirty years earlier. In the end, the necessary funds were collected, and at the beginning of the summer a field party returned to the camp below the feet of the stone columns.

The first order of business in 1922 was a brief reconnaissance of the upper San Juan drainage around Pagosa Junction to the southeast of Chimney Rock and along the Pine River to the west. In the first locality local diggers previously had unearthed samples of crude black-on-white pottery from pithouse depressions sprinkled over several acres. Along the Pine near the modern Ute agency at Ignacio, recent Anglo and Native American activity had disturbed older remains of what seemed to have been cobblestone or adobe structures and a scattering of discarded fragments of earthenware, grinding tools, and debitage. Although no excavations were done, the survey confirmed a widely distributed ancient culture in some respects similar to and probably contemporaneous with much of that at Chimney Rock.

At the focal location on the Piedra River, exploration was initiated at three groups of mounds on the first east terrace above the river. One group was on a spur of the foothills to the north of the Pagosa-Durango road. Two additional mound complexes were a couple miles south of the Harlan ranch, where work had been carried out the previous summer. Discoveries at two of these places elaborated on the earlier findings of adobe and cobblestone pithouses and sandstone-slab upper walls resting on cobble foundations. The third site consisted of surface rooms whose masonry of coursed thin and thick blocks was not unlike that of the Chimney Rock pueblo. In his report on this ruin, Roberts, who had returned for a second time, speculated that it was of a late stage in the

Black-on-white vessel in the shape of a mountain sheep with an upturned nose taken in 1922 from a burial at a site at the western base of the Chimney Rock mesa. A handle originally attached the head to the body. One ear is partly broken off. The wavy lines are thought to represent fur. A solid triangular element with a negative stepped central motif runs down the back. Specimen stands 8.25 inches in height and is 6.5 inches long. *Courtesy Colorado Historical Society.*

local sequence. This judgment was considered likely in future work, not just because of the advanced type of construction but also because ceramics retrieved from three burials were finer. These included a charming black-on-white hollow figurine of a mountain sheep, some black-on-white bowls with expertly drawn, more compact patterns, and jars of what were then called "coiled ware." Such pottery later was termed "corrugated" and determined to be an innovation of the Pueblo II stage of development (see Chapter 3). A tiny piece of turquoise taken from one burial further suggested to researchers at that time a temporal placement postdating the pithouse culture.

In all the terrace settlements dug to that date no structure that could be regarded as a kiva as defined elsewhere on the Colorado Plateau was

Partially excavated Chimney Rock pueblo, ca. 1922. East kiva is in foreground. Figure in background may be J. A. Jeancon. *Courtesy Colorado Historical Society.*

exposed. However, there was a frequently repeated pattern of circular depressions banked on at least two sides with low swales. Conceivably, these once might have been subterranean ceremonial chambers, each with its complement of surface user dwellings. The larger of these depressions were suggested to have been open-air plazas or courtyards where community dances took place. For the time being, definitive answers to these matters were put aside for future inquiry.

Back at the Chimney Rock pueblo on its lofty perch above the guardhouse, work continued in the row of cubicles between the two kivas and in the west kiva itself. Here some standing walls comprised eleven feet of coursed masonry, making excavation quite a different job from trying to trace the often elusive outlines of the shallow floors and crumbled cobblestone walls of the structures down in the valley. The walls in the west part of the Chimney Rock edifice were not as well

A large duck-shaped jar recovered in pieces in 1922 at the Chimney Rock pueblo further convinced Jeancon that this site was somehow related with those in Chaco Canyon. Because of the use of a vegetal pigment, later research suggests an origin somewhere in the neighboring northwestern San Juan area. *Courtesy Colorado Historical Society.*

constructed as those in the eastern portion, implying an earlier building episode. Large accumulations of refuse were deposited within them, suggesting that this series of chambers had become a communal dump for a considerable period of time before the final abandonment of the rest of the village. The western kiva lacked some of the features found in its eastern counterpart, but it did have a raised firebox and a southern ventilator shaft. The latter did not have an attached horizontal floor-level tunnel. Part of the kiva floor had been put over a bed of sand used to smooth the uneven caprock subsurface. Charred fallen timbers indicated a cribbed roof structure. Unfortunately, dendrochronology was an unproven means of dating in 1922, and bits of beams and other building timbers, as well as chunks of charcoal, were removed and tossed aside. Jeancon felt confident that he had found an outpost of Chaco culture, writing in 1924, "The result of the studies at Aztec and Chaco show that the Chimney Rock people were undoubtedly related to both of these areas. Similarity in pottery designs and forms, masonry, and house plans establish their relationship."

Within a few months after excavations ceased at the Chimney Rock pueblo, the old house began to deteriorate. The covering of fallen rocks and timbers and wind-deposited earth protecting it for centuries had been removed. Recognizing the problem, Jeancon advised the U.S. Forest Service to undertake immediate preservation measures. He observed that these would be time-consuming and expensive; water needed to mix cement mortar for re-laying walls would have to be hauled by burro more than a mile from the Piedra up the steep trail to the site. Recognition of these twentieth-century difficulties underscored the tremendous amount of effort that had been expended by the aboriginal builders, who lacked beasts of burden and canvas water bags or wooden kegs to help them get water to the heights.

As Jeancon pointed out, an alternative method for supplying water to the modern masons would be to build a road. With improved access, other ruins could be repaired more easily and the entire complex could be set aside as an archaeological preserve for public visitation. Baring an undercurrent of professional jealousy that has plagued the science since its inception, Jeancon wrote that he hoped it would be a state park rather than being added to the young national park system because he felt that Jesse L. Nusbaum, superintendent of Mesa Verde National Park, would adamantly oppose continuation of the Society's work. Jeancon need not have worried. The Chimney Rock pueblo was not repaired, a road was not built, and the Colorado legislature had no interest in proprietorship of a state park.

The next year, Jeancon sent out a survey headed by Frank Roberts that included Roberts's brother, Henry, and two friends. It was his first solo effort in the field, and quite surely he felt his oats. He was young and undaunted by the assignment Jeancon gave him: locating all prehistoric remains over varied terrain stretching 150 square miles from where the San Juan River gushed down out of the Rockies to its passage through the arid lands at the Utah border. A preliminary examination the previous season had produced promising results. Roberts equipped his little expedition with two Model T Ford touring cars and piled grub boxes, shovels, tents, and other paraphernalia in the back seats and on the running boards. He and his companions decked themselves out in the stereotypical exploration attire of the times — knee-high laced

Frank H. H. Roberts, Jr. *Smithsonian Institution photo 92–6038.*

boots, riding breeches, and felt campaign hats. This equipment was a step down from the pith helmets, swaths of mosquito netting, and phalanxes of colorful native workers characterizing the popular view of archaeologists being nurtured by Sunday newspaper photogravures of "lost cities" and King Tut's tomb (opened just a year earlier). Nevertheless, an air of romance attached itself to even such a humble venture in the U.S. West.

Departing from Pagosa Springs in mid-June 1923, the two-car convoy bounced over the dirt road going south along the western plateaus rimming the San Juan. Roberts wisely stopped at each of the cultivated patches belonging to the Archuletas, Aguirres, Gallegos, Quintanas, and other Hispanos to inquire whether in the course of digging ditches, installing fencing, or tending flocks of sheep the owners might have noticed Indian ruins or relics; if so, he and his colleagues would like permission to examine them. Everyone, it seemed, knew of something

Ducks share a 1923 Roberts farm camp. *Courtesy Colorado Historical Society.*

relevant and was eager to tell of it. Passing along from family to family, the Roberts party slowly made its way westward from the bend of the river at the hamlet of Trujillo, where the first ruins were observed. Sometimes the diggers camped overnight in the settlers' yards, where drinking water and shade were available.

At summer's end, Roberts and his team had placed hundreds of archaeological sites on their maps. Work concentrated on the tributaries as far west as the Animas, beyond which other investigators had made earlier reconnaissances. The remains recorded were of three types. One set of remains came from a relatively brief, limited intrusion of Navajos and Pueblos following the temporary expulsion of the Spaniards from the northern Rio Grande Valley at the end of the seventeenth century. The other two resulted from an extensive prehistoric occupation along the main course of the San Juan and its principal laterals. These sites appeared to correspond to that at the base of the Chimney Rock cuesta. Older and more numerous, these remains were characteristic of what was then being called the Pre-Pueblo horizon: low, heavily eroded mounds that Roberts thought resulted from decay of pithouses. Some were found in the floodplains, where they had been churned up by modern plowing. More often they were isolated on successive terraces retreating back from the watercourses. Many of these were at a considerable distance from the water. Beneath the sage covering these mounds, the surveyors noticed many clods of burned adobe and scattered fragments of pottery and broken stone tools. Without digging, Roberts decided that the dwellings mantled by the accumulation of burned soil had been constructed with the jacal method, in which spaced vertical posts are sealed into thick layers of mud. Conspicuous depressions of up to sixty feet across were either in the center or to one side of the mound clusters. Less frequent were disintegrated surface buildings made of courses of sandstone slabs or cobbles held together with masses of adobe mud.

Two observations were particularly intriguing because they paralleled similar features on the Chimney Rock mesa. On a point of Montezuma Mesa, rising abruptly from the riverbed of the San Juan and allowing a vast horizon-to-horizon vista, Roberts happened onto a spot in the rocky surface where huge conflagrations once had occurred. At a short distance was a ruin mound. He could not but wonder if the burn area had been a signaling station for the neighboring village and if it might have been part of a communications network reaching as far north as Chimney Rock. Flames or smoke could not have been seen directly between these two locales, but perhaps in the unexplored intervening wilderness there was another station. The other feature of special interest matching one on the Chimney Rock mesa top was a small circular cup very obviously cut into bedrock of Haystack Mountain near the town of Allison. Both bowls were about half a foot deep. In neither instance were there signs that the holes had been used as grinding mortars. Whatever other purpose they might have served remained a mystery.

More recent vestiges of the past were the sixteenth-century or early-seventeenth-century forked-stick hogans attributed to the Navajos and the rectangular coursed-masonry rooms perched on top of impregnable heights believed to have been erected by Rio Grande Pueblo peoples hiding from Spanish overlords. Sherds picked up in some of these places suggested that Jemez Pueblo residents had lived in them. Petroglyphs carved into cliff faces were identifiable as the work of Navajos, who prior to the Roberts survey were not known ever to have moved north of the San Juan River. The archaeological team also found clues to a period of European influence — settlers showed them yucca fiber ropes braided in typical Spanish fashion and a beaten copper plate.

The greatest concentration of ruins was found in the Piedra River valley. From the confluence of this stream with the San Juan, where the community of Arboles grew over a group of pithouses, north to where the valley pinched down at Chimney Rock, an unbroken line of pithouse mounds and heaps of stone houses stood on east and west benches. Also observed were several examples of Navajo or Pueblo occupation and rock art dating to the late seventeenth century, as well as probable nineteenth-century Ute camps. The men saw a masonry complex with standing six-foot-high walls on a high ledge to the west of the river opposite Chimney Rock and another on the crest of Coal Hill to its south. Both sites were reminiscent of and probably coeval with the houseblock up by the pinnacles. Thirty mounds spread over the flat plateau of Stollsteimer Mesa southwest of the Chimney Rock cuesta hinted at rather sizable Pre-Pueblo villages and seemed to Roberts to be potentially important in rounding out the prehistory of the district.

The next summer Roberts again spent three weeks doing some superficial digging on Stollsteimer Mesa but was called upon to finish the areal survey before much was accomplished. Four years passed before he returned to the Piedra area.

Meanwhile, Jeancon was back on Devil Creek in 1925 after a disappointing fund drive. He was discouraged with a legislature that annually promised and then withdrew research allotments and a lack of public appreciation for regional archaeology. In spite of the mounting

Unexcavated ruin mound on Stollsteimer Mesa, ca. 1924. At right rear, an abandoned pole-and-mud structure originally may have been erected by an early-day Hispanic settler. *Courtesy Colorado Historical Society.*

evidence for important aboriginal habitation in the upper San Juan region, no sites had been found with the glamorous appeal of the Mesa Verde cliff dwellings or the tumbled-down apartment houses baking in the sun of Chaco Canyon. Such sites might have spurred substantial financial contributions. The Chimney Rock pueblo was the sole contender for headlines, but it yielded few of the material things that curators and interested laymen equated with significance. Data was merely for the ivory-tower types — or so Jeancon concluded as he pondered resigning his position at the State Historical and Natural History Society.

In 1925 Jeancon and a crew of local workers trenched one of the round depressions frequently found near house mounds. When cleared, the sunken space was some six feet deep and twenty feet in diameter. Large river cobbles ringed the depression, which was paved with stones covered with a thick layer of hard-packed adobe. A fire hearth was centered on this floor. From the lower level a five-foot-wide terrace sloped up to an encircling bank, or bench, which in turn graded up to ground level. Jeancon's typescript of the excavation does not mention any evidence for a superstructure of walls and roof. Rectangular one-roomed dwellings with slightly sunken floors and post-and-mud walls were immediately adjacent. Jeancon interpreted the site as a pithouse village with a dance courtyard, which he called the "Plaza Grande." His informal paper notes, "The whole mesa top, on which Plaza Grande is situated, is almost a solid mass of ruins, mostly of the fourth period. Associated with Plaza Grande proper are two, or possibly three, more

View toward the west showing the 1925 clearing of the site containing Jeancon's "Plaza Grande" on a tongue of the Chimney Rock cuesta, with Petersen Mesa rising beyond the Piedra River. *Courtesy Colorado Historical Society.*

circular areas which appear to be the same sort of thing. No excavating was done in these places. There are also many detached single and double houses as well as several fairly large groups, one of which was excavated in 1921."

On the second terrace above the Harlan ranch, the party explored a second so-called tower. It possessed the same dimensions, cobblestone walls, and interior embellishments as the structure dug out in 1921. Instead of being isolated, as was the first construction, this one was associated with small cobblestone and adobe rooms and placed in a strategic spot controlling access to some trails up the Chimney Rock cuesta. The pottery recovered was primarily utilitarian ware. Jeancon described it as being bullet-shaped, with coils laid up in a wavy indented manner and furrowed perpendicularly by the potter's fingers. Future researchers named this ceramic type "Payan Corrugated" and found it typical of the late archaeological phases of the upper San Juan Basin.

In 1927 the Pecos Conference, a gathering of forty-five individuals then engaged in research dealing with some aspect of the prehistoric Southwest, worked out a standardized terminology and developmental sequence that helped place the Piedra district antiquities in their proper relationship to others scattered across the Colorado Plateau. Roberts, who attended that conference, had just excavated a pithouse village at the eastern end of Chaco Canyon, which he confidently placed in the newly defined Basketmaker III stage. He believed that with further exploration on Stollsteimer Mesa, he could bring the cultural record forward in time to the next stage, formerly called Pre-Pueblo but now

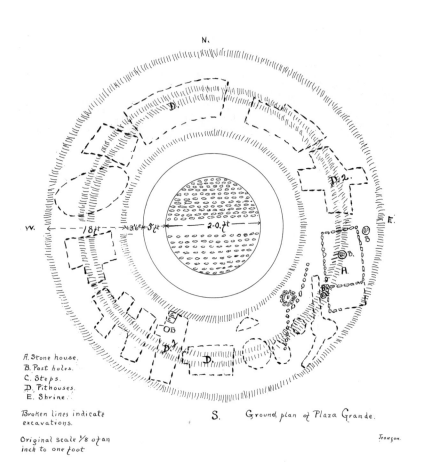

A. Stone house.
B. Post holes.
C. Steps.
D. Pithouses.
E. Shrine.

Broken lines indicate
excavations.

Original scale ⅛ of an
inch to one foot

S.   Ground plan of Plaza Grande.

Jeancon.

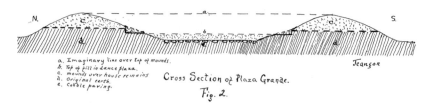

a. Imaginary line over top of mounds.
b. Top of fill in dance plaza.
c. mounds over house remains
d. Original earth.
e. Cobble paving.

Cross Section of Plaza Grande.

Jeancon

Fig. 2.

Previously unpublished Jeancon drawing of his 1925 excavations at the lower Chimney Rock cuesta site containing what was then described as a dance plaza. *Courtesy Colorado Historical Society.*

Cleared basal walls of cobbles and mud of what Jeancon in 1925 interpreted as a tower structure. In center foreground are several milling bins containing metates and manos. The Chimney Rock pinnacles are visible at left rear. *Courtesy Colorado Historical Society.*

designated as Pueblo I. Therefore, the digging season of 1928 saw him back where his archaeological career began.

During the four-year interval between visits to Stollsteimer Mesa, Roberts had spent two seasons in Chaco Canyon for the National Geographic Society expedition, finished a doctorate in anthropology at Harvard University, and taken a job at the Smithsonian's Bureau of American Ethnology in Washington. Jeancon carried out his threat to resign from the State Historical and Natural History Society, by then renamed the Colorado Historical Society, and his successor, Paul Martin, moved field operations to the Four Corners. With government money available and other professional claims on the territory eliminated, Roberts secured permission to work on the Southern Ute Indian Reservation, of which Stollsteimer Mesa was a part. He hired a local Hispanic crew and plunged into a prodigious excavation program. By the end of the summer eighty dwellings, two kivas, six circular depressions, and seven cemeteries had been explored.

Three related but distinct architectural types were present in the villages. Roberts considered them sequential: two were of the Pueblo I horizon, and one evolved into early Pueblo II. Entire communities into which these house types were clustered had burned either during occupancy, upon abandonment, or in the ensuing centuries. In some cases, it appeared to Roberts that the residents had been caught by the flames just after a fall harvest. Pots filled with corn kernels, beans, and various seeds lined the walls. Because the devastation was so complete, he felt it was evidence of warfare. The fires so hardened the earth partially or

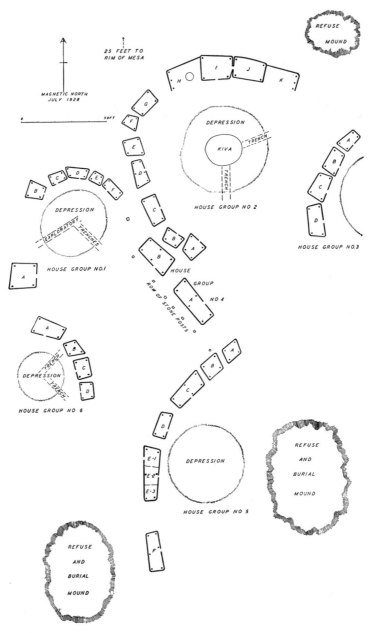

Drawing of Pueblo I village on Stollsteimer Mesa. *After Roberts, 1930, Plate 3.*

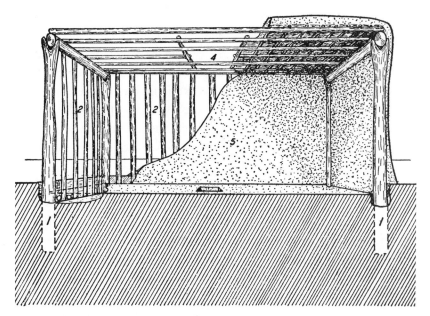

Roberts's reconstruction of an early Pueblo II jacal house type on Stollsteimer Mesa. In sequence, his numbers indicate main support posts, small wall poles, roof timbers, opening for smoke hole, and mud-plastered wall. *After Roberts, 1930, Figure 6.*

totally encasing wooden frameworks that beam impressions were retained, providing an accurate picture of construction. One-room quadrangular to rectangular detached surface units were the rule. Walls were of jacal, with some lateral door openings in them. The doors themselves were large stone slabs. Roofs were flat, made of posts and brush covered with earth, and pierced with a central smoke hole directly over a fire hearth on the floor. In the two earliest types, floors were cupped a foot or so into the surrounding surface. Some exceptionally small rooms with no ground-level door or hearth were probably storage chambers. In the most recent dwelling style, the storage rooms were made of unshaped rocks set in large amounts of adobe. Roberts saw these structures as the first local attempts at masonry.

The typical settlement pattern was a crescent around or near a yawning depression that, Roberts suggested, resulted from digging and puddling the huge amounts of earth needed for this kind of construction.

He came to the conclusion that most of these pits became reservoirs trapping runoff from rains and snowmelt. Because the villages were a considerable distance above either the Piedra River or Stollsteimer Creek and because no aboriginal trash was dumped into the pits, the reservoir hypothesis seemed plausible. Roberts found no evidence to support Jeancon's idea that the depressions were dance plazas. Trenching revealed only two instances where the Indians had converted the pits into what may have been early versions of a kiva. More likely, they were pithouses.

As usual in sites situated in the open, pottery was the most abundant type of recovered artifact. Having just completed a masterful analysis of Chaco ceramics for his dissertation, Roberts devoted a second study to those of Stollsteimer Mesa. He found that architecture and pottery together delineated the Pueblo I and early Pueblo II periods there. Many of the characteristics the Pecos Conference listed as diagnostic for those periods were obvious in this sherd lot: coils in neck areas of utility jars, rather than being obliterated, were retained for decorative effect and reinforcement; white slip was used to mask gray body ground; vessel shapes were more varied and larger; painted designs were timid and poorly drawn in early phases but grew bolder and more elaborate through time; and corrugated exteriors of cooking and storage receptacles were introduced.

The benches beside the Piedra held not only the physical remains of numerous prehistoric settlements but also the bones of their occupants. In layered fashion, that testimony of life and death carries through to modern times: the Hispanic village of Stollsteimer impinges on a Pueblo I dwelling group, and the Catholic chapel and its cemetery cover a midden used as its burying ground.

Elsewhere, the crew unearthed more than one hundred human skeletons in refuse mounds within each village precinct. For religious reasons the ancient Piedra dead were buried within trash deposits, composed of daily discards. Death was regarded as a continuation of the human cycle, and it was not considered disrespectful to inter them with the physical goods of earthly life. Furthermore, the trash deposits afforded easier digging with a stick than hard, compacted ground. Generally bodies were buried in flexed positions and sometimes accompanied

Pottery vessels recovered from Pueblo I–early Pueblo II sites on Stollsteimer Mesa: a) undecorated seed jar with eleven holes around orifice, possibly for insertion of feathers; b) bag-shaped utility jar with corrugated base and unindented coiled upper body; c) white-slipped small bowl bearing encircling black decoration executed in mineral pigment. *Courtesy Colorado Historical Society.*

Pottery vessels recovered from Pueblo I–early Pueblo II sites on Stollsteimer Mesa: a) black-on-white canteen; b) black-on-white pitcher; c) corrugated seed jar; d) undecorated dipper; e) plain utility jar. *Courtesy University of Denver.*

with simple offerings. Most skulls had been artificially flattened in infancy to produce the broad-headed Puebloan profile. At that time the few not so treated were considered a resilient Basketmaker strain.

Occasionally graves yielded mystifying or intriguing results that made excavators yearn to reach across silenced generations. One was a small pit into which had been wedged two male skulls and four earthenware vessels. What could possibly have been the tragic story behind this burial? Were the men victims of crime, accident, or warfare? Were they killed during a hunt far away from home, making transport of their entire bodies too burdensome? Another burial of special interest was that of a man who obviously had been a person of consequence in the community. He was interred with a cache of well-made projectile points, bone-knapping tools, twenty-one pieces of pottery, red ochre, and the bones of a golden eagle.

Years and the elements of nature had distilled the transitory presence of hundreds of individuals in the Piedra district into a pitiful few stumps of walls, bits and pieces of imperishable objects used to get from day to day, withered foodstuffs that even rodents or weevils had ignored, and the terminal contribution of human bones. Even with such an incomplete assemblage of evidence, at the end of what was to be his last field endeavor in the region, Roberts felt his work had illuminated a few pages of the earliest chapter of Pueblo life. It was a confused time when change from the Basketmaker mode to something more elaborate was taking place. The surveys and digs substantiated a shift from the deep pithouses used elsewhere to slightly depressed to above-ground chambers, from jacal to masonry architecture, from detached to contiguous rooms in linear plans. Additionally, a cultural advancement similar to that others were exposing on many adjacent arteries of the San Juan was identified. It was generally agreed that at some period in the past, people pursuing a lifeway categorized as Pueblo I spread throughout this fertile but demanding part of Colorado. The Piedrans had neighbors in other drainages. Perhaps jacal architecture remained in vogue longer in northeastern sectors because of plentiful timber supplies and a scarcity of easily fractured stone. Perhaps some small handicrafts, such as pottery, did not evolve as rapidly there as in other parts of the northern Southwest because geographical isolation and small-scale occupation denied artisans the stimuli of crossroads centers. Still, it seemed to Roberts and his contemporaries that across the Colorado Plateau the ancients somehow had marched through time in relative cultural unison. It would not be until the year after research on the Piedra ceased that dendrochronology began to supply calendar dates that set the record straight.

3

ANASAZI UNDER WATER

Water is an enemy of antiquities. Yet, paradoxically, the threat of impounded water proved to be a boon to the unraveling of the prehistory of the upper San Juan district.

In 1956 Congress enacted legislation to construct the Navajo Dam on the San Juan River as part of the Upper Colorado River Storage Project. A lake some thirty-four miles long was expected to back up behind that construction to the 6,100-foot elevation contour, flooding the lower Pine River canyon and spreading approximately six miles north and east of the merger of the Piedra with the main stem of the San Juan. Ten lesser side channels also were to be inundated. The dam's inlets, outlets, spillways, diversion tunnel, and coffer dam would further disturb the natural topography. By the 1950s the environmental movement had gained sufficient strength to demand the recordation or recovery of whatever archaeological or historical resources might be submerged before they were sacrificed forever on the altar of modern irrigation and recreation needs. Because the area to be most affected lay in New Mexico, the Department of the Interior contracted with the School of American Research and then the Museum of New Mexico, both in Santa Fe, to do the job. Dr. A. E. Dittert, Jr., served as director.

The location of the San Juan uplands on the border of the Anasazi world and the absence there of large structures, other than the unique Chimney Rock pueblo beyond the reach of the Navajo Reservoir, had doomed them to virtual archaeological oblivion following the pioneering work of Frank Roberts. But multiyear government funding provided the impetus for scientific examination of a previously ignored region, where a human presence was suspected to have been in place for many

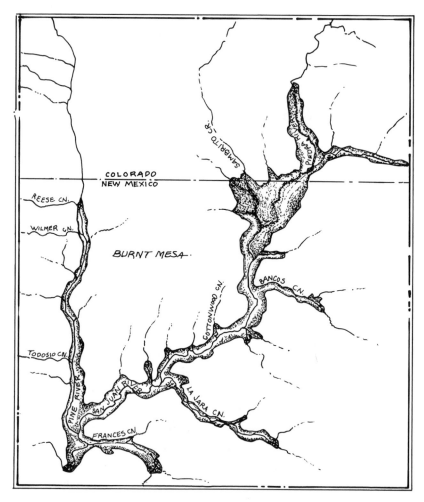

Map of Navajo Reservoir on San Juan River and tributaries in relation to Chimney Rock Archeological Area. *Courtesy U.S. Forest Service.*

centuries prior to the arrival of white dam builders. From 1957 through 1962 teams of archaeologists and support personnel took to this field, with another three years devoted to laboratory analysis and reporting. The results helped explain the background of the Chimney Rock prehistory.

Archaeological reconnaissance in rough terrain lacking an adequate road network was not without its problems. Getting from here to there

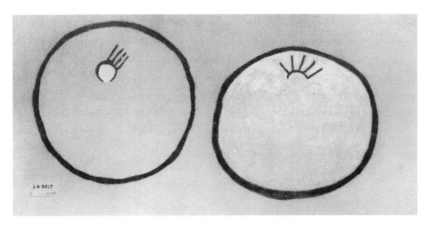

The concept of the Twin War Gods, depicted in a now-submerged pictograph on a cliff beside the San Juan River (Site LA 3017), was borrowed by modern Navajos from the Pueblo Indian cosmology that possibly was rooted in the Anasazi past. *After Schaafsma 1963, Figure 36.*

often meant slogging step by step. Surveyors were transported to a drainage mouth and picked up hours or days later at its head. In summer heat they plodded up and down embankments, forded and reforded rocky streams with boots dripping wet and feet threatened with fungus, tramped broad sagebrush flats, and laboriously scrambled to lofty mesa tops as they meticulously scanned the ground for bits of telltale evidence of former occupation. The lower canyon of the Pine was particularly troublesome because its narrow, sheer-walled gut defied access. The resourceful men then converted the museum field jeep into an amphibious craft by attaching a vertical extension to its exhaust pipe; it might get hung up on a rock, but with luck it would not drown. One can only wonder at what the astounded aborigines would have thought of that noisy monster charging upriver past their stumpy hillocks of corn struggling to grow on the narrow benches above the water.

Work commenced near the dam site because extensive borrow operations in the bed and terraces of the river would be needed to get material for what was then to be the second-largest earth-fill dam ever built by the Bureau of Reclamation. In the first season thirteen prehistoric sites were excavated and forty-seven others were noted as ravenous equipment sat ready to move in and devour them. Eventually, nearly seven hundred places where ancient people had hunted, lived, worked, or died were plotted on a field map, twenty-one of which were either cleared or tested. Artifacts discarded from this parade of life were processed. A huge file of photographs was compiled. Panels of rock art pecked into or painted on cliff faces were recorded, among them Navajo depictions of the Twin War Gods. Evidence for perhaps five or more millennia of man's habitation of the upper San Juan corner of the Colorado Plateau had been obtained.

PALEO-INDIAN, ARCHAIC PERIODS
CA. 3000 B.C.–A.D. 1

The Museum of New Mexico party did not find Paleo-Indian lithic remains within the Navajo Reservoir pool confines, but they have since been recovered in small quantities in nearby areas. Evidence from adjacent parts of the San Juan Basin suggests that ancient hunters wandered there in search of large game, primarily bison, for some thousands of years before the Christian Era. Eventually environmental changes led to a decrease in the size of the bison herds, causing the nomads either to drift eastward toward the grassy Great Plains or modify their basic food-gathering patterns in order to sustain themselves otherwise. In the case of the latter adjustment, they slowly developed a way of life typifying the Archaic period.

In the Navajo Reservoir district the Archaic was characterized by a few thin deposits of hearth litter (rock that had been splintered by fire), earth discolored by disintegrating charcoal, fragments of projectile points, and a scattering of pecked and ground stone implements. The limited number of Archaic use zones, restricted to mesa crests in the southern sectors of the dam project, suggested intermittent wandering bands of people with a low-level technology for gaining and preparing the wherewithal for daily survival. The projectile points spoke of a diet of small fauna, and the milling stones would be used to grind leaves, stems, berries, and wild nuts. Finds in other regional Archaic sites indicate that maize corn may have been grown there as early as 1000

B.C. but probably in a restricted way that did not interfere with the more important seasonal foraging. The San Juan drainage cut through upland and lowland terrain suitable for a combination of the two fundamental life support systems, horticulture and hunting-gathering. However, as the cultivation of corn assumed greater significance because of its predictability, the need to stay full-time in one place increased, and seminomadic Archaic bands metamorphosed into the sedentary Anasazi.

LOS PINOS PHASE (BASKETMAKER II) CA. A.D. 150–400

At about the same time the Romans were tossing Christians to the lions on the other side of the world, some players emerged from behind the scenes of the earlier shadowy Paleo-Indian and Archaic periods to commence a thousand-year run on the San Juan stage. By the time Rome was sacked, these men and women already were firmly committed to a revolutionary shift away from rootless nomadism to a lifestyle increasingly anchored by simple horticulture and sedentism. Somewhere else, maybe along the foothills of the San Juan Mountains, they had learned how to plant kernels of corn and squash seeds to produce important supplements to whatever undomesticated edibles were available. With growing seasons of up to 150 days in length and a perennial water supply, the floodplains and terraces beside the San Juan corridors offered a favorable microenvironment. Somewhere else, these people cleverly had learned to create shelters for themselves out of the earth, rocks, and timbers around them. This, too, may have been part of a cultural growth that took place a short distance away.

Researchers working with these particular San Juan remains referred to them as examples of the Los Pinos Phase, or Basketmaker II as defined in the Pecos Classification. At first, the lower Pine River region seemed the center of this occupation, but later investigation put the heartland further north, near the small modern community of Bayfield and closer to a second comparable development in the environs of Durango. The term "phase" implied that it was one step in a long cultural evolution by a single physical stock. After the mid-1930s the entire prehistoric continuum on the Colorado Plateau was called "Anasazi" rather than being split into Basketmaker and Pueblo categories. Regardless of the stage taxonomy devised to artificially order data, there was no sharply defined delineation between one period of development and the next but rather a subtle growth process.

The earliest of the regional prehistoric dwellings, recorded at twenty-three sites, were situated on the edges of benches above the floodplains through which the few watercourses flow. The novice farmers of the era presumably prepared and tended garden parcels down below, where there was arable land and little arboreal vegetation. In those locations the plants benefited from runoff trickling down the cliffs, seasonal flooding of the river, and high water tables near the streams. The randomly scattered one-room houses were either vaguely circular, circular with a small rounded antechamber separated from the main room by a hallway demarked by rows of upright poles, or figure-eight in shape. Their earthen floors were slightly scooped below ground level. Exterior dwelling walls were made of dry-laid cobbles leaned against a cribbed wood framework or of river cobbles held in vertical position by wads of adobe mud over a foundation of logs placed in a channel gouged into the ground. Bands of stones ringing a few structures were first thought to have been a purposefully installed paving, but most likely they represented fallen walls. The builders created some interior partitions with closely spaced upright wooden timbers, stuffing the interstices with worn basket fragments and corn cobs, which then were encased with mud. Because the diameter of the units averaged some twenty-seven feet, roofing them demonstrated an impressive degree of practical engineering skill. The feat probably was accomplished with horizontally laid cribbed logs secured in position by nothing more than placement and weight to form a dome or truncated superstructure with a central smoke hole/entryway. Occasional indications of trouble loomed overhead, where irregularly placed holes in the dirt floor indicate, it is believed, where emergency vertical roof braces may have been installed.

Pits of various forms pockmarked the floors. Some were smoothed with mud that hardened, others were rimmed with sandstone slabs, and

Los Pinos Phase (Basketmaker II) Albino Village pithouse (Site LA 4269),
upper Pine River section of the Navajo Reservoir district, with encircling ring
of cobbles. *Courtesy Museum of New Mexico.*

still others were untreated. Several above-ground cupboards were fash-
ioned from concentric coils of mud, gradually tapering in circumference
to make a beehive form. Fire-reddened walls suggested that excavated
pits with a restricted mouth and undercut sides may have been the
Crockpots of the day. Sandstone slabs or clay plugs sealed various cists
from rodents, who would recklessly have gambled on escaping the
cooking pits. These humble pits, and others found outside the houses,
reveal two important qualities of this period. First, gathering and/or

Schematic drawing of cut-away and roofed pithouse. *Courtesy U.S. Forest Service.*

farming yielded surpluses needing to be held over from one season to the next either as seed stock or as foodstuffs. Second, thought was given not only to living today but continuing to exist tomorrow. The ability to look to a future, however clouded, was a clue to the cultural progress of the first more-or-less settled inhabitants of the upper San Juan.

Crude as the dwellings were, they were a major advancement over open-air camps. They afforded protection and must have been reasonably comfortable cocoons in winter, with fire basins, body heat, only one exterior opening, and the insulating properties of earth and stone. However, open hearths and exposed wooden roofing elements turned them into fire traps. Some seasonality in their use is possible, and the term of tenure may have been brief. Nevertheless, the considerable energy invested in the erection of the domiciles points to their having been regarded as permanent.

The bulk of portable manufactured objects from the Los Pinos Phase ruins were of stone. They exhibited able craftsmanship in their formation and performed a wide range of functions. Spear points, blades, and choppers were used for hunting, skinning out the bag, and butchering it for consumption. Game animals probably were dispatched by an atlatl and spear. Deer, with their taste for the plentiful scrubby browse of the mesa tops (now locally called buck bush), were the most likely targets. Scrapers and knives were made for working hides, and grinding slabs and hand stones for pulverizing corn and wild seeds. Their proportionately high number reflects the importance of gathering and small-scale horticulture. Hammers, abraders, and cores were the tools needed to form other stone implements; drills, scrapers, and choppers cut and shaped wooden objects; and round cobbles helped smooth and compact construction mud. Sharp-pointed bone awls served in the preparation of articles of animal hides and in the weaving of baskets. Baskets themselves were not recovered intact because exposure in open settings obliterated the remains, but a number of impressions of them were observed on hardened clods of adobe mud applied as part of the jacal construction.

Pottery was absent from the artifact assemblage at these sites except in late horizons, when a few pieces of brown wares apparently began to be produced. They were among the earliest earthenware made in the northern Southwest.

A few collapsed walls, several hundred stone artifacts, and impressions of corn cobs in fire-hardened adobe or corn pollen found near several burials constitute a paltry index to several hundred years or more of human activity. By drawing analogies with modern peoples, one can speculate on the hard-earned cumulative environmental knowledge that enabled the group to survive or the nonmaterial artistic expressions that permitted it to enjoy doing so. However, several finds among the meager residue of the Los Pinos Phase possibly shed light on activities less fundamental than those employed in preparing internal body fuel and external body warmth. A few unembellished bone beads and several tablets on which red or green minerals for pigment had been crushed attest to the vanities of personal adornment and body painting. Two dog burials in which hapless canines had been severed in half and interred affirm the practice of ritualistic sacrifice.

The Navajo Reservoir archaeologists attempting to reconstruct Los Pinos Phase life placed it between A.D. 1 and 400. A combination of dating techniques such as archaeomagnetism, radiocarbon analysis, and ceramic stylistic variation has allowed a refinement in dating that for some researchers shortens the period to between A.D. 150 and 400. Statistical studies based on the number of occupied zones, square footage of structures, and probable size of extended familial units produced a population estimate of less than three hundred persons overall in the Los Pinos Phase. Probably some habitations were overlooked because of faint surface indications, and the average size of nuclear families may have been greater than the base figure of three-plus individuals used in the reservoir study. Nevertheless, individual generational numbers over two and a half centuries appear to have been small.

Most of the Los Pinos dwellings were isolated units where a family lived near the land it tried to tame and cultivate. Four concentrations of a half-dozen houses in close proximity may be antecedents to the later established pattern of settled Pueblo village life. These groupings may have been used and reused over time rather than as permanent villages. The cultural stage as a whole was part of a more extensive distribution of eastern Basketmaker II people ranging southward from the vicinity of Durango, along the Animas River valley, and southeast across green uplands to the Pine. Still further east, the twin pinnacles of Chimney and Companion rocks overlooked a river valley far removed from where the action was. It remained quiet and unviolated.

Meanwhile, back near the Navajo Dam locale, the Los Pinos population either gradually dwindled away or sharply declined in number. Over centuries their post-and-cobblestone houses slumped back to earth.

Sambrito Village being excavated during the summer of 1960. *Courtesy Museum of New Mexico.*

SAMBRITO PHASE (BASKETMAKER III)
CA. A.D. 600–700

With a cultural revitalization, people again reappeared on the banks of the San Juan, and they chose to settle in what would become the middle reaches of the modern reservoir just south of the Colorado–New Mexico state line. They obviously regarded the front edges of broad Pleistocene benches lining the river as suitable for dry farming. Moisture from subsurface water and summer rains was sufficient to nourish their gardens. Whether or not the newcomers may have been migrants moving out of the Mogollon Mountains several hundred miles to the south, as was originally postulated, they carried some important cultural traits associated with that region.

Among the new introductions was a house style in which basal walls were the sides of a pit. The incentive for builders equipped with nothing more that long stout sticks, baskets, and an enormous application of

Deep pithouse in Sambrito Village (Basketmaker III, Site LA 4169) on a terrace above the San Juan River at its former confluence with Sambrito Creek. A central hearth, wing walls, floor cists, and ventilator shaft are typical features for the period. This pithouse was part of an extensive occupation at the site extending from ca. A.D. 400 to 1000, with a Navajo use of the same locale probably in the 1700s. *Courtesy Museum of New Mexico.*

human muscle to burrow commodious round holes three to four feet down into stubborn rocky soil is not as hard to explain as it might seem. First, southern influence may have been infiltrating northward about the seventh century; more important, the adoption of the true pithouse had a practical ecological basis. The tree cover needed for wall logs was thin to absent in many places on the Colorado Plateau, but dirt was

54

everywhere. Furthermore, digging-stick excavation actually may have been no more laborious than felling timber with cumbersome stone implements or fire and then manually transporting the heavy beams to construction localities. And, as people in arid environments worldwide have discovered, earthen architecture tends to be cool in summer and warm in winter. With most living activities assumed to have taken place out of doors, houses primarily were havens from inclement weather or for sleeping.

The first San Juan pithouses were relatively small and shallow, with the same interior characteristics as the earlier Los Pinos log-and-cobblestone structures. Floors were mud plastered, sloped up cuplike to meet mud-plastered walls, and were riddled with various storage holes, post depressions, pot rests, and a central hearth. Benches for storage or for sleeping were cut from pit sides. Ventilation to allow fresh air in and stale air out was achieved by a vertical slot opening at ground level gouged out of the encircling earth. In small houses, access and egress was achieved by means of a ladder through a smoke hole over the central fire basin; in larger dwellings, a ramp from ground level into an entry antechamber was used. Roofs probably were low and truncated; timbers leaned up against a square center beam frame to form the slanted upper walls of the pit, and the whole affair was covered with a thick layer of earth.

Even though exterior wall construction was modified, the preference for a circular floor plan and the general pattern of usage remained the same as it had been in the previous centuries of semisettled life. Parents, children, and possibly a grandparent all shared one enclosed living space. Probably two or three generations of related families were accommodated in more spacious units. In some cases, these greater structures may also have been gathering places for integrative social or religious group functions. Outside was an associated array of underground cists, which excavator Frank Eddy interpreted as baking ovens. At one locality, forty-five such subterranean undercut pits were discovered. They were found accidentally when a bulldozer operator scraped the ground to reveal an unsuspected complex of pit mouths crowded into a confined area. Several of the so-called ovens were found to have doubled as convenient crypts for human remains and the carcasses of

Overview of a concentration of Sambrito Phase (Basketmaker III) fired cists excavated in 1962. They were dug into a spur of land on the east bank of the San Juan River half a mile above its former junction with the Piedra River. Contemporary and later houses were in the vicinity. *Courtesy Museum of New Mexico.*

dogs severed in half. Even in this Stone Age culture, few were foolish enough to dig with a stick when it was unnecessary.

A second major addition to the cultural inventory was pottery. The ideas for its manufacture are thought to have passed along from central Mexico to reach the Mogollones, whose homeland straddled what are now the international Mexican-U.S. borderlands of Arizona and New Mexico, about the time of Christ. From that place and time, the concept of pottery making reached outward in ever-widening ripples and was adopted by diverse peoples, who at the same time were embracing sedentism, for which pottery was appropriate. The earliest pottery samples from this second period of San Juan occupation are a crude but polished ware. Because it is brownish in color, researchers earlier speculated either that pottery was traded from southern Mogollon to northern Anasazi along some commercial network or that Mogollon potters may

Small, undecorated, brown utility pottery recovered from the Sambrito Phase (Basketmaker III) type site: a) bowl; b) spouted bowl; c and d) jars. *Courtesy Museum of New Mexico.*

have been among those who took up homesteads on the San Juan. Recent reanalysis shows that local alluvial clays rich in iron content and a firing process then used by novice potters that allowed limited oxidation explained the brown coloration, rather than any outside influence or artisans. The vessels often were begun in a basket. Coils of clay then were added upward and welded together through finger pressure and scraping, then smoothed by a hard-edged object, perhaps a chunk of dried gourd rind or a piece of broken pottery. Basket impressions were retained on some vessel bottoms.

Undoubtedly pottery greatly facilitated the household chores of storage, cooking, and eating. For convenience, water could be kept in the dwellings. Without glaze for waterproofing, some evaporation through the walls of storage jars occurred, but this process kept the contents of the vessels cool. Dry foodstuffs could be kept in small containers without requiring another cist in the floor. The availability of heat-resistant, semi-impervious receptacles promoted new culinary procedures. After hundreds of years of a dry diet of raw plants, parched seeds, roasted corn, and rare bits of skewered meat grilled over a smoky fire, more liquid preparations, such as gruels, stews, and herbal teas, must have been gastronomic delights. It is noteworthy that the growing of beans, a final cultigen added to the standard triad of prehistoric Southwestern domesticates and whose preparation necessitated boiling, was somewhat contemporaneous with the introduction of pottery.

The first vessel forms were small, round-bottomed jars, some with necks, and bowls having indrawn orifices. These could well have been cook pots that would have nestled down into an open hearth and whose contours helped to hold in heat. Fired clay items in divergent shapes were for other purposes. These included circular spindle whorls used in weaving and objects, such as a bird effigy and short conical pipes, with possible ceremonial functions.

A complement of stone and bone implements was retrieved. Among these artifacts were small stone projectile points suitable for tipping arrows, fragments of juniper bark matting, and scraps of basketry. Particularly intriguing were a few ornaments, including pendants, beads, and bracelets, made from Pacific shells. With the source of the shells hundreds of miles away from this ancient dry-land outpost on the San

Juan, the jewelry confirmed the existence of long-distance trade channels. Finished items were special enough to be fitting offerings for the
dead.

The archaeologist in charge of these excavations judged the remains
to be from the Basketmaker III horizon. In accordance with the San Juan
chronology developed by project personnel, he called this the "Sambrito
Phase." Basing his opinion on a combination of stratigraphic and ceramic dating methods and a few radiocarbon dates, he believed it fell
within a three-hundred-year interval, from A.D. 400 to 700. Consequently, in his opinion the Sambrito Phase represented a vital connecting link in the local continuum between the Basketmaker and Pueblo
time frames. If so, then there was no gap in occupation in the district,
as was believed prior to the Navajo Dam archaeological work.

Not all colleagues agree with this assessment. One opinion is that
some of the dates are not relevant and that there was a hiatus of perhaps
two hundred years between the Los Pinos and Sambrito phases. Another
is that the Los Pinos and Sambrito phases were more compressed in time
than the reservoir crew would have them and that they overlapped to
such an extent as to be one evolutionary period rather than two distinct
ones. The estimate of a mere fifty to sixty individuals living over a span
of three centuries in just seven sites of uncertain contemporaneity also
casts doubt on the validity of this phase. However, most Sambrito sites
experienced subsequent occupations, which may have obscured some
underriding Sambrito materials. There well may have been a more
extensive population than the survey actually identified.

ROSA PHASE (EARLY PUEBLO I)
CA. A.D. 700–850

Some time in the early eighth century there was a land rush to the
upper San Juan. The archaeological team found a string of sites that had
been lived in at that time stretching the entire distance of the proposed
reservoir. The heaviest concentration of pithouse ruins was just south of
the New Mexico–Colorado state line, where the landforms were not as

rugged as those closer to the dam site. For the first time the Anasazi had discovered the broad flat valley at the confluence of the Piedra and San Juan rivers. Estimates are that the population increased twentyfold over that of the preceding Sambrito Phase. Even so, with 225 individuals per generation spread over a varied tract of land thirty-four miles long, congestion was not a problem. However, this population estimate may be too low.

Where did these people come from? The most logical source is the Gobernador drainage flowing into the San Juan network from the southeast. Work there just before World War II demonstrated a flourishing late-Basketmaker III–Pueblo I occupation, in many respects not unlike that on the San Juan. Tree-ring analysis established construction dates of the Gobernador in the late 700s through the 800s for a period the archaeologist termed the Rosa Phase. At the same time, a notable augmentation of Anasazi numbers occurred in other sectors of the northern periphery of the Colorado Plateau. It would seem that settled existence supported by a growing emphasis upon agriculture led to a prehistoric baby boom.

A second question is: Why did the Anasazi move into a region that apparently held little appeal earlier? One reason may have been a simple overflow from a nearby center of development, where desirable lands were at a premium. Because the Gobernador district had no permanent rivers, perhaps the perennial waters of the San Juan and the broader floodplains in the upper reservoir pool area acquired new value with increased gardening. Also, some of the Gobernador settlements were encircled by defensive post stockades; the potential for raiding may have prompted movement into more secure canyonlands.

The original areal survey and subsequent excavation of sixteen Rosa Phase sites in the reservoir preserve showed the dominant settlement pattern to be isolated single pithouses, some away from the riverine settings, with a few grouped into hamlets. There were a greater number of units at each village than in the Sambrito Phase, as required by the presence of more inhabitants. The semisubterranean dwellings were larger than those of the Sambritos, dug deeper although still relatively shallow, and had more structured ventilator shafts and full or partial benches. A few boasted a *sipapu*, or ceremonial floor opening to the spirit

Excavations at late Rosa to Arboles phases (Pueblo I–early Pueblo II) Sanchez Site situated near the former juncture of the San Juan and Piedra rivers. The Hispanic community of Arboles, Colorado, in the background now lies beneath the waters of the Navajo Reservoir. *Courtesy Museum of New Mexico.*

world, possibly indicating that, in addition to being domestic houses, these were places of cult activities. Some homeowners had had enough of digging-stick excavation and built rectangular surface rooms of jacal for living and storage. Refuse either was thrown around the premises, most typically on the downhill slopes, or dumped into the nearest flowing water. In randomly scattering shelters and trash, the locals deviated from the custom of their contemporaries in other districts. Whether that was by choice, laziness, or ignorance of what was expected is a tantalizing question.

Although some brown pottery continued to be produced, the gray wares that were to characterize Anasazi output for the next six hundred years made their appearance in considerable abundance. Earthenwares had become indispensable furnishings. The gray base color resulted from the firing process: pots were baked over smothered flames, which reduced the amount of oxygen in the atmosphere. It is not known why potters chose to follow this method, but it made Anasazi pottery unique in the ancient Southwest.

Most vessels were hard and rough-textured. Those intended for storage or cooking increased in size over what they had been in Sambrito times and were left plain. However, unobliterated coils of necks of some jars reinforced a vulnerable part of the pot, at the same time adding a decorative touch. This neck-banding became a hallmark of Pueblo I. Open serving bowls were also made, and with them came the introduction of crude painted decorations. A pigment that fired black was derived from boiling down parts of plants, such as the tansy mustard and Rocky Mountain beeweed. This process obviously could not have been undertaken prior to the existence of receptacles in which to cook liquids and solids together — in short, because the Rosa Phase housewives had pots, they then could decorate them. A less frequently used pigment was made from a pulverized lead mineral. This fluxed, turned greenish, and partially vitrified under low temperatures.

Some pottery traits, such as the green lead-glaze pigment, were generally out of date elsewhere by the eighth or ninth centuries. The production of gray ware, the use of painted decoration, the application of slip, and the making of open bowls and other forms seem to have become part of the technology of these artisans later than in other parts of the Pueblo I sphere. This lagging development underscores the marginal geographical situation in which this society operated. There would always be a backwoodsiness about the upper San Juan Anasazi.

The archaeological record indicates that Rosa Phase participants were increasingly committed to horticultural pursuits. Campsites on the floodplains were interpreted as places where farmers stayed while tending fields. Numerous hafted stone axes were thought to have helped clear land and build houses. Fewer projectile points and stone knives were recovered from the principal sites, a sign that hunting was not as important as it had been. More manos and metates for grinding and more vessels and baskets for storage reflected increased production of foodstuffs needing to be processed and stowed away. Rosa Phase Anasazi had culturally adapted to their environment.

Their existence remained a hardscrabble one. Still, a general cultural enrichment is demonstrated in a greater variety of stone, bone, and shell objects, some of which were imported from outside the immediate region. A few luxury items were present, such as hairpins, whistles, and shell and gilsonite jewelry. Conspicuous consumption was occasionally displayed in burials, where a cache of two dozen pieces of pottery might be placed in a single grave for an individual with a degree of social standing.

With a modicum of success in horticulture, the Anasazi quite surely became concerned about assuring its continuation. That meant religion. From the time men planted the first seeds to bring on the Neolithic Revolution, they fretted about the weather and felt at the mercy of a myriad of little-understood natural forces. The rains that did not come, the hail that wounded gardens, the hot winds that seared the soil, and the late frosts that turned seedlings brown and limp were seen as the actions of supernatural beings who had to be placated with ritual offerings and prayers. The few material clues to that side of early Pueblo thought are some pottery effigy figures of ducks and fish — both associated with the crucial natural element of water — clay cloud-blower pipes, and stone corn-goddess symbols. The bizarre slaughter of man's best friend, a trait also observed in the Gobernador remains, seems to have been done for other reasons.

Despite whatever rites may have been performed around the *sipapus*, the Rosa Phase Anasazi were threatened with a natural disaster at the middle of the ninth century. One of the recurring cycles of riverine down-cutting, which for eons had chewed the Colorado Plateau and spit it out in the Gulf of California, began again. Because of major shifts in climatic patterns, the San Juan River steadily became more deeply entrenched in its middle sections, where the gradient was greatest. That, in turn, drained away the subsurface water that nourished tender roots of Anasazi corn, beans, and squash. The lands on which those plants grew were left high and dry, and surrounding terrain suffered a reduction in vegetational cover.

One can visualize the elders, squatting on their haunches around the hearths, debating what to do. What they did was what they had done before and would do again: they moved. Demographic shifts were a way of life for the Anasazi as a means of coping with a country only marginally suitable for agriculture. If the nutrients of thin soil were exhausted or precipitation patterns changed where they were, the Anasazi farmers found another place to try again. Many of the thousands of former settlements that dot the northern Southwest probably were lived in for only a decade or two. The forced relocations may not have been particularly traumatic. Although it meant starting over, generally no great distance was involved, and the neighbors, houses, their arrangements on the landscape, and apparatus for living remained much the same. The Anasazi householder was not bothered with transporting a plethora of unnecessary things.

So it was that around A.D. 850 the lower ten and a half miles of the reservoir district were abandoned as the San Juan Anasazi migrated to greener pastures. They could not head south because there was a dearth of good farmland in the barren slopes of the Chaco Plateau. To the west a heavy population along the La Plata drainage already had usurped the best areas. Northward the frost belt fronting the San Juan Mountains presented too many subsistence obstacles. So they went upriver ahead of the entrenchment, keeping to a riverine/low upland environment and becoming further isolated from their contemporaries in the lower San Juan Basin.

PIEDRA PHASE (LATE PUEBLO I)
CA. A.D. 850–950

Coincident with the progress of the Navajo Reservoir excavations, archaeologists came to accept the use of heavy earth-moving equipment to clear sites of sterile overburden accumulated through centuries of deposition. Consequently, a backhoe, operated by an archaeologist fully aware of the cultural composition of the sites being examined, skinned off the crusty surface and dug bucket-sized trenches through promising sectors to provide a profile of the zone. Occasionally the backhoe exposed subsurface dwellings that were undetected from the surface. A great amount of time and effort was saved by this mechanical aid. Once the peek beneath the earth's rind was afforded, researchers quickly decided whether or not the site might add new data to fit into their long-term study goals. When the decision was made to continue excavation, crews from the local Hispanic communities took to their shovels and trowels, just as they had done in Roberts's day.

In the ninth and tenth centuries, the lifestyle of the greater numbers of upper San Juan Anasazi became more fixed into a static highland tradition distinctive from that evolving at Chaco Canyon to the south or in the Mesa Verde region to the northwest. Most peoples of this era, called the Piedra Phase by the excavators, continued to live in single-unit pithouses of several styles dispersed along the terraces above the river, but there were more of them per square mile than previously. At the mouth of the Piedra River where the stream meandered through rich silts, forty sites were noted, twenty-nine of which were occupied during the Piedra Phase, or late Pueblo I. A preference for utilization of Recent terraces rather than higher Pleistocene benches confirms the need to tap lower water levels. The walls of some Piedra Phase pithouses were reinforced by poles to forestall slumping, but otherwise their style differed little from that of their ancestors. The Piedrans constructed one or a linear series of rectangular jacal rooms on the ground surface nearby. The fact that some were outfitted with fire hearths shows them to have been used for living rather than for storage. The jacal rooms generally had cobble or sandstone foundations and occasional cobblestone paving to discourage burrowing rodents. Trash was thrown in a heap off to one side. In general, the remains in the lower Piedra Valley resembled those that Roberts had explored thirty years earlier in the northern portion of the valley.

Because of the gradual movement upriver, several villages that had been inhabited in earlier times expanded in size. The largest, located on the west bank at the confluence of the San Juan River and Sambrito Creek, consisted of ninety-one identifiable units. Judging from architectural features and datable ceramics, nineteen pithouses, thirteen surface structures, and five exterior pits were left from the Piedra Phase residency. That appears to have been the peak period of use of the community, because during the next epoch only a single pithouse was lived in. By the early 1000s it, too, was vacated. Eight hundred years later Navajos moved in to erect four forked-stick hogans adjacent to the almost obliterated pit depressions. These more recent inhabitants undoubtedly salvaged surviving useful artifacts discarded by their predecessors.

An enrichment in the sociopsychological life of the Piedrans may explain the digging of an extra large pithouse in each locality having a concentration of smaller structures. The grandest of all had more than fifteen hundred square feet of floor space. The roof probably was supported by six large posts arranged in a circular pattern about the floor. An encircling bench and an absence of floor features were notable. These "super-pithouses" likely served as community centers for the village and outlying satellite homes. Based upon indirect evidence, some usage of a religious nature can be assumed. For example, clay effigy figures of fish or waterfowl, a cone-shaped stone regarded as a corn-goddess fetish, and presumed medicine kits containing exotic rocks or fossils may have been cult goods for ceremonies held in such places. Having large ceremonial or gathering rooms as part of a settlement cluster was the rule rather than the exception in most contemporaneous Anasazi quarters located on the eastern and northern Colorado Plateau. The Navajo Reservoir archaeologists called theirs Shabik'eschee kivas, after a Great Kiva dug in Chaco Canyon by Roberts. However, the huge pit structures of the Piedra Phase lacked any direct ties to Chaco itself; they merely represented a widespread sharing of a cultural phenomenon.

Although substantial finds of corn cobs and kernels, squash rinds, and beans suggest successful harvests, and although faunal remains can be interpreted as discards from fruitful hunting forays, the general economy may not have been flourishing. Cultural growth stagnated. Despite some refinements in stone tools and increased mastery of the craft of pottery making, there were few major additions to the repertoire of material things. Trade goods were limited. Moreover, the Piedra Phase was a period of reduced rainfall and shorter growing seasons. These factors, added to the continued headward erosion of the river, probably made suitable farmland scarce and harvests uncertain. Conflicts may have erupted within the group over food supplies and perhaps over the ineffectiveness of religious leaders in assuring their abundance. In addition, the resident population may have clashed with outsiders, who also might have been affected by adverse conditions.

There is some confirmation of turbulent times on the San Juan during the ninth and tenth centuries. Several of the larger villages were surrounded by stockades of upright posts wedged into position by stones. Although one opinion is that the stockades were meant to confine turkeys, they may have reflected a perceived need for defense. A clue to trouble on the San Juan came from one pithouse that contained the long bones and skulls of twelve individuals. The long bones had been fleshed and opened while green, with interior marrow scraped out. After being cannibalized, the bones were tossed on the floor and the house above set on fire. In other dwellings human skeletal remains also had been incinerated. Just as on Stollsteimer Mesa, many structures had burned. Certainly strife brought on by extreme desperation is a possibility.

ARBOLES PHASE (EARLY PUEBLO II)
CA. A.D. 950–1050

The northeastern Anasazi may have fought each other, but they could not fight Mother Nature. According to one interpretation, year by year the San Juan River hungrily ate into its bed and borders, further lowering the critical water table and devouring potential farmlands. Even runoff-water farming, wherein fields were cultivated at the outlets of channels or arroyos, proved risky. A conflicting view is that about A.D. 1000 the San Juan River valley experienced high water tables and aggradation that brought on flooding of the valley floor. Regardless of the underlying causes, people slowly migrated upriver and gathered together into small communities. For a century fewer than several hundred persons remained near the mouth of the Piedra and eastward along the base of Sandoval Mesa, which forms the north cliff of the San Juan River.

The Arboles Phase people, or Early Pueblo II in the traditional classification, continued to reside in the pithouses that had become customary for the region. On occasion they also erected linear rows of surface rooms made of sandstone slabs laid horizontally in thick beds of mud, the first attempts at masonry on the upper San Juan. They were what Roberts called "Type C construction" on Stollsteimer Mesa. These units were floored with cobbles. Other surface structures were of jacal over cobble foundations. Excavators uncovered some evidence for temporary brush *ramadas* which could have been used for outdoor workplaces. In pottery manufacture, the participants of the Arboles Phase adopted use of white background slip for painted vessels and relatively infrequent corrugation on exteriors for gray wares. The latter were pinched spirally, a distinctive surface treatment. The vessel forms to which it was applied were baglike and different from anything in the rest of the northern San Juan area.

ANASAZI UPRIVER

In the late 1960s and early 1970s there was a postscript to the Navajo Reservoir archaeological project. E. Charles Adams, then a graduate student at the University of Colorado, undertook a study of Anasazi settlement patterns along the San Juan drainages upriver from the lake created by the Navajo Dam. The area encompassed 45,000 square acres of the Southern Ute Indian Reservation in Archuleta County southeast of Chimney and Companion rocks and north of the San Juan River. Adams confirmed a cultural expression comparable to that within the reservoir pool and tabulated 147 sites ranging in date over a three-hundred-year period from A.D. 750 to 1050. From about A.D. 850 on, these proved to be remains resulting from ecological pressures downriver. Over time, these pressures forced northeasterly migration toward the foothills of the Rocky Mountains, where Cat Creek Ridge formed a natural 8,000-foot-high boundary rimmed with sandstone.

Adams's work coincided with the inception of the computer age in Southwestern archaeology. He focused on statistical analyses of data in order to understand why and how the Anasazi settled in and adapted to diverse environmental niches within this locality and ultimately forsook them. Through these means Adams concluded that all the usual explanations for settlement — i.e., carrying capacity of lands as a result of agricultural modifications, cold air drainage into narrow valleys, population growth and consequent stresses, social, economic, or political activities, transportation routes, natural defensive features, and the need or potential for new foodstuffs — were by themselves too narrow in focus. All, however, likely contributed in some way to site distribution.

The carrying capacity of what Adams termed the lower Piedra district (although the Piedra River valley was not included) in any one phase was 308 individuals. Using an arbitrary figure taken from ethnographic analogy (i.e., comparison with modern Native American communities) of six individuals per pithouse, he found that at no time were there more persons present than the district could support. Adams estimated a population during the Rosa Phase (A.D. 750–850) of 210 persons, or one-third less than the maximum. They lived in dispersed single-family pithouses in riverine terrace settings near arable lands, and their development was coeval to that on the lower San Juan; they were not there because of the misfortunes that later came to pass in the Navajo Reservoir district. Horticulture still being a part-time affair, these Rosans had little need for many additional storage facilities.

The Piedra Phase (A.D. 850–950) saw a peak district population of 258 persons, who continued to dwell in pithouses but often clustered them in the uplands, where higher elevation and greater precipitation meant annual soil moisture was more evenly distributed and the principal crop of maize had a better chance of flourishing. Typically these Piedrans also built jacal or limited-function surface structures in locations where wild foodstuffs could be procured, stored, and processed. Some of these settlers had indigenous roots, but others migrated into the district because of environmental changes downriver.

During the Arboles Phase (A.D. 950–1050), the number of people present declined to an estimated 120 because of movement out of the district resulting from a decrease in the amount of tillable land. The actual size of the pithouse settlements increased as people came together to more fully exploit what riverine locations there were. Jacal surface units were placed next to plots of farmlands, enabling individuals to claim and more efficiently work them.

Ultimately, environmental conditions deteriorated to the point that further adaptations in order to maintain cultural stability were no longer possible. Beginning a little after A.D. 1000, a migration out of the main upper San Juan territory began. Those who went southeast across the

Continental Divide in New Mexico likely formed the population out of which the Gallina culture evolved several centuries later. Those who drifted ten or eleven miles up the Piedra Valley linked with contemporary Chimney Rock communities, the evidence of which Jeancon and Roberts first used in 1921 to launch regional archaeology. They formed a stranded enclave on headlands in the shadow of the rocks.

ANASAZI EXPOSED

A quarter of a century after the Navajo Reservoir archaeological project terminated, a second chance to reexamine some of the submerged antiquities unexpectedly arose. In 1987, when the dam was being repaired, the water level was drastically reduced to the point where prehistoric sites once again were exposed and a human skull at one of them caught the attention of boaters on the lake. The Bureau of Reclamation contacted Complete Archaeological Service Associates of Cortez, Colorado, to recover what eroding human remains were evident and conduct salvage excavations where warranted.

The skull came from a burned pit at the lower edge of a clay ridge that had extended underwater from the shore near the junction of the San Juan and Piedra rivers. The archaeologists assumed the location to be the Basketmaker III Oven Site excavated by Frank Eddy in 1962, where he had noted an unusually dense concentration of subterranean cists. Because fires obviously had reddened their interiors, Eddy concluded that they had been used for roasting animal or plant foods. No remaining particles of those foods were recovered, however, nor were there any associated fire-cracked rocks that might have been used to conduct heat.

Nancy and Larry Hammack, owners of the contract archaeological firm involved in 1987, and their crew determined that the newly exposed pit was one of a complex of an additional twenty-three similar constructions situated upslope from the Oven Site. The pits were identical to those at the Oven Site, making a total of sixty-eight known cists in the immediate vicinity. They acknowledged a strong probability that others

The 1989 excavation of storage cists at the Oven Site (LA 4169) first examined in 1962. *Courtesy Complete Archaeological Service Associates.*

are there in many suitable spots along the former river terraces, which are no longer visible.

The cone-shaped pits were gouged by digging sticks about three feet down into a deep bank of clay, which formed the feature walls. The floors had diameters of three to nine feet and were flat. Pit mouths were restricted and had been sealed with thin, large, worked sandstone slabs that, after abandonment, had slumped into the interior fill. All but one of the pits had been burned prior to being used, which hardened the clay walls to an imperviousness sufficient to thwart rodent and insect activity and moisture seepage. The sandstone covers showed no comparable fire reddening. Taking all these factors into consideration, the Hammacks viewed the pits as terra-cotta subterranean storage silos rather than ovens.

Whether the burned pits were used for cooking or for warehousing, their number emphasizes great success in farming and foraging and indirectly hints at a larger residential population than was first postulated. A dating technique called archaeomagnetism (wherein iron particles in

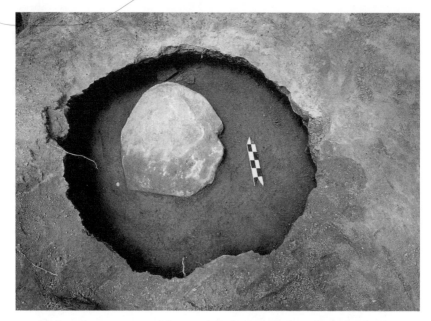

Looking down into one of the complex of sixty-eight large, burned, subterranean cists at the Oven Site dating from the seventh century. The stone was a roughly shaped lid, the surrounding mouth of the cist having eroded and fallen into the pit. *Courtesy Complete Archaeological Service Associates.*

burned clay are measured for their alignment with known positions through time of the magnetic north pole) worked out in the years between the Navajo Reservoir archaeological project and the recent salvage work confirms construction in the late sixth or early seventh centuries. The Sambrito Phase span defined by Eddy thereby is verified.

At a later time, the pits were used as tombs. Single burials were found in five of them — it was the skull from one such grave that alarmed the Bureau of Reclamation in 1987. Bodies were laid out on pit floors and covered with fill dirt rich with the remains of wild and domestic plants. Associated ceramic offerings were indicative of the late Sambrito Phase.

To determine whether other sites within the pool area were being similarly impacted by wave action or fluctuation of water levels, the crew took to a pontoon boat to survey the shoreline. Eerily, after being sunk for so many years, stone rings around sixteen-hundred-year-old pit structures reemerged from their watery grave and were clearly visible on slimy mud flats. Around them, heavy stone objects that had been left where found in the 1960s were still in place, but all lighter sheet trash and spoil dirt taken out of the excavation area had washed away. No further skeletal materials surfaced.

Now all that is left of these Anasazi and their material accomplishments is safely back underwater. The lake impounded by the great earthen Navajo Dam has drowned the ghost towns of perhaps a thousand years of Anasazi history. Yet the cultural record might never have been so fully reconstructed had it not been for the modern water needs of the Navajo Nation and ultimately the conglomerates of Phoenix and Los Angeles.

(a) View over stabilized walls of the Chimney Rock pueblo toward the modern fire tower and the two pinnacles in the background. *Courtesy Jim Fuge*.

(b) Sunrise over Chimney Rock. *Courtesy Jim Fuge*.

(c) View of Chimney Rock from southwest flank of the San Juan Mountains. *Courtesy Jim Fuge.*

(d) The trail from the ruins of the Chimney Rock pueblo runs west down a ridge of the Chimney Rock cuesta toward the Piedra River valley in the distance. *Courtesy Jim Fuge.*

(e) Aerial view of the Chimney Rock pueblo. *Courtesy Jim Fuge*.

(f) Aerial view of the excavated Chimney Rock pueblo roomblock and two kivas. *Courtesy Tom McMurray.*

(g) Aerial view to southeast over the Chimney Rock pueblo, the pinnacles, and San Juan Mountains in the distance. *Courtesy Jim Fuge*.

(h) The two Chimney Rock pinnacles from which the site derives its name. *Courtesy Tom McMurray.*

4

ANASAZI IN THE BACKWATER

For nearly fifty years the excavated portions of the Chacoan pueblo on the uppermost crest of the Chimney Rock mesa lay bare. Decay began almost immediately upon the departure of the diggers from the State Historical and Natural History Society. Rains pelting against the exposed masonry slowly dissolved the mud mortar. Freezing and thawing pried veneer from its rubble core backing. As a result, large sections of walls collapsed into heaps of sandstone blocks and were covered with windblown dirt and tumbleweeds. As Jeancon had warned in 1922, a vulnerable Anasazi ruin was becoming ever more ruinous.

Finally, in 1968, administrators of the San Juan National Forest initiated efforts to reclaim this neglected cultural resource before it was too late. They signed a contract with the Mesa Verde Research Center, a field station of the Department of Anthropology at the University of Colorado, to clean up the derelict houseblock and excavate associated sites on the cuesta. An archaeological preserve of 6.12 square miles was to be set aside for public inspection. Beginning the ensuing summer and continuing for the two following seasons, teams of student archaeologists under the direction of Frank W. Eddy, who had been a primary field researcher in the Navajo Reservoir Archaeological Project, toiled on the Chimney Rock mesa. They cleared formerly dug sections of the large structure and excavated one room, the previously untouched part of the east kiva, and the east and south courtyards adjacent to the building. As they finished, a crew of Navajo workers specially trained in ruin-stabilization procedures reset stones, capped walls, and tried to secure the house's future well-being. Their supplies of sand and cement were

Chimney Rock pueblo as it appeared before 1970s' stabilization. *Courtesy San Juan National Forest.*

brought to the site by helicopter, and a water line for mixing mortar was run up the mesa.

Additionally, the researchers examined four complexes of structures lower on the mesa: the so-called guardhouse on a spine of rocky land below the primary pueblo and three others near the terminus of a road the Forest Service was building up the south escarpment. They also made a survey of the entire precinct down to the waterways on three sides of the landform in order to determine the kind and extent of prehistoric occupation that had occurred and its probable temporal relationship to the crowning pueblo at the base of the twin pinnacles. This gathering of data has allowed a series of related studies that continue to the present.

To first consider the story revealed on the upper Chimney Rock mesa is like reading the last chapter of a book before working through the preliminary digitations of the plot. Anasazi pioneers laid the groundwork for later developments on the Chimney Rock mesa during the second half of the ninth century or a bit later, moving out of the main San Juan River artery because of untenable conditions and making their way up the Piedra Valley. Frank Roberts encountered evidence of their arrival and settlement on terraces lining the tributary Piedra River and on the

Collapsed room walls of Chimney Rock pueblo prior to stabilization. *Courtesy San Juan National Forest.*

Excavators trench rubble accumulated over an earth-paved courtyard along the south wall of Chimney Rock pueblo (Site 5AA83). *Courtesy University of Colorado.*

Stollsteimer Mesa that fronted the river on the east. They clustered detached and contiguous rooms around large man-made depressions, which Roberts thought were merely borrow pits for mud mortar but others now suspect may have resulted from caved-in community pit structures. He reported no single-unit pithouses on Stollsteimer Mesa but considered the jacal rooms to have provided year-round shelter and storage.

Just prior to the 1970s' work on Chimney Rock mesa, a group of university students under the direction of Robert H. Lister conducted

West kiva of the Chimney Rock pueblo, showing condition of walls prior to 1970s stabilization. *Courtesy University of Colorado.*

an archaeological survey of adjacent Southern Ute Indian Reservation lands. This survey included parts of the upper Piedra Valley, Stollsteimer Mesa, Lake Capote at the eastern foot of Chimney Rock, and the highlands west of the Piedra River. The surveyors encountered the by-then familiar pithouse depressions, rock alignments of circular or rectangular rooms, burned adobe clods and posts left from jacal structures, rock art, and areas without architectural features but covered with stone flakes discarded during projectile point and tool manufacture. These signs of former human presence were at elevations centering on 7,000 feet. The team also excavated a Pueblo I pithouse in the vicinity

Stabilized walls of rooms and west kiva. *Courtesy San Juan National Forest.*

of the Southern Ute agency at Ignacio on the Pine River. It conformed in style and content to the finds of coeval sites throughout the northeastern San Juan region. More recent surveys have reaffirmed a cultural sequence across the wedge of uplands between the Pine and Piedra rivers comparable to that along the San Juan River, with a notable withdrawal toward the northeast.

Once the University of Colorado team began its survey of the Chimney Rock Archeological Area of the national forest, it found extensive Piedra Phase (late Pueblo I) occupation on terraces bordering the river. Pithouses of several sizes accompanied by jacal surface structures laid out in bars or L- or U-shapes were characteristic. Excavation is needed to know whether they were deep or shallow.

These various undertakings confirmed that as population pressures increased throughout the tenth century because of the influx of people dislocated from the primary San Juan drainage to the south, a major movement to the very head of the Piedra Valley occurred. This migration brought the Anasazi to the environmental limits for their maize-

Trail, or causeway, down the cuesta spine from the Chimney Rock pueblo toward the guardhouse ruin. *Courtesy San Juan National Forest.*

Archaeologists clear overgrowth from a mounded site (5AA92) about to be destroyed in 1970–1971 by road construction up the south side of the Chimney Rock mesa. *Courtesy University of Colorado.*

based horticulture and into a ponderosa pine, piñon, and juniper vegetational zone. Elevations ranged from 6,400 to 6,700 feet in the floodplain and on the benches along the south and north slopes of Chimney Rock mesa, where lower temperatures prevailed than in the regions from which they had come. Moreover, cold air settled in the relatively narrow upper Piedra Valley, and the prominences on the east and west horizons blocked the sun's warming rays except at midday. These factors were responsible for a shortened growing season for maize that hovered precariously around the 110 to 120 days necessary for maturation. A slight climatic change meant probable crop loss. However, there were advantages to the new setting: a sandy loam soil suitable for the raising of maize; broad, relatively flat areas that could be cleared and cultivated; a permanent water supply in the river and increased precipitation because of the proximity of the high mountains; reduced evapotranspiration, keeping soil moist; and accessible resources such as timber, stone, clay, and wild foodstuffs.

Northwesterly view from the crest of the Chimney Rock mesa toward the upper end of the Piedra Valley. Terraces descending to the river were densely occupied by Anasazi of the Piedra and Arboles phases (late Pueblo I–early Pueblo II). *Courtesy San Juan National Forest.*

Life for the tenth-century Arboles Phase (early Pueblo II) Anasazi on the upper Piedra proved satisfactory. Their numbers multiplied. Particularly on the toe of the Chimney Rock mesa overlooking the juncture of the Piedra River and Devil Creek, they congregated together in villages composed of pithouses and small surface units of a few adjoining rooms built of various combinations of jacal, cobbles, and sandstone slabs. Several towers in addition to those explored by Jeancon and Roberts were present, as were assorted roasting pits and storage cists lined with sandstone. Without excavation, it is impossible to know if the numerous large depressions near these identifiable structures were remains of community ceremonial rooms, oversized domestic pithouses, or a mixture of both.

Just as the architectural conventions that evolved over centuries of occupation on the upper San Juan remained relatively constant, so too

Unexcavated sites on the terraces above the upper Piedra River, of probable early Pueblo II age, appear as scatters of stone slabs from fallen walls. *Courtesy San Juan National Forest.*

did those of material culture. The comparatively small but varied yield of artifacts included a few stone objects such as manos, metates, mortars, axes, polishing and abrading stones, lap anvils, pot lids, scrapers, gravers, hammers, and drills made from local river cobbles. Projectile points were common enough to suggest that hunting was an important activity. Pottery was represented primarily by a limited number of restorable gray vessels and a random assortment of fragments from others. Black-on-white potsherds came almost exclusively from simple bowls. Occasional corrugated texturing on utility jars and broad-lined designs on service vessels are probably signs of a widespread sharing of basic ideas among all northern San Juan Anasazi rather than direct influence from any one specific source, such as Mesa Verde.

The picture that emerges from analysis of Piedran architecture and material culture is that these were ultraconservative people who moved out of the reservoir area and became increasingly cut off from meaningful contact with Anasazi living elsewhere on the Colorado Plateau who

Vessel shape and surface texturing identify this utility vessel as a type named Payan Corrugated, whose styling was to continue into later occupation of the Gallina area of north central New Mexico. *Courtesy Marcia Truell Newren.*

might have brought innovations to the local lifestyle. Such interaction as did exist took place with those who lived due south of the San Juan in the Gobernador area and followed a comparable cultural pattern. Trade items, other than a very small amount of obsidian from the Jemez Mountains and farther south in New Mexico, are scarce. Mountain nomads of undetermined affiliation may have exchanged hides and wild foods for pottery.

Those wild foods, whether traded for or gathered by hand, expanded the diet beyond the corn and bean cultigens. Especially in hard times, the biologically rich mountain environment prompted a dramatic return to a hunting-and-gathering subsistence base more characteristic of the opening eras of the Anasazi continuum. Modern flotation methods, in which buckets of soil are subjected to water separation to extract fossilized pollen, indicate that rose hips, serviceberries, chokecherries, wild currants, sunflower seeds, and prickly pears were gathered in season. A few wild species, such as lamb's-quarters, probably were allowed to colonize garden plots. Curiously, the piñon nut–juniper berry–oak acorn assemblage typically a part of the native plant communities was not found by paleoenvironmentalists in the retrieved materials. This absence probably was due to a sampling problem.

As for hunting, elk, mule deer, bear, mountain sheep, and other large game were bagged. Bones of smaller animals further indicate a diversified meat component to the diet, as well as an abundance of bone resources for tools and adornment, and furs and hides for apparel and other uses. The small fauna include porcupines, beavers, muskrats, otters, grouse, squirrels, marmots, turkeys, mice, rabbits, rats, coyotes, weasels, badgers, and foxes. Here, as well as elsewhere on the Colorado Plateau, fish appear to have had little importance as a food resource.

Based upon the estimated number of rooms in the concentration of habitations on the lower north slope of Chimney Rock mesa, the primary zone of occupation, and hypothesized components of three to five individuals per family, Eddy put the population at that locality at between 624 and 1040 persons. These figures likely are too high and greatly exceed population estimates for any period in the Navajo Reservoir district. Still, some growth inevitably increased the grouping of dwellings and the size of villages. This concentration may have been a way of meeting the circumstances of a challenging environment. In efforts to feed the populace, full exploitation of the available arable land undoubtedly ensued. It was just a matter of time until the overflow had to expand onto new lands.

The Stollsteimer Valley, coming into the Piedra along the southeastern side of the Chimney Rock mesa, presumably attracted development after A.D. 1000. It was relatively broad and flat, more open to sunlight, with highly productive soil and a permanent stream. Farm plots are thought to have been cleared along the valley floor and at the mouths of ravines cut into escarpment faces on either side, but the people using the area chose not to live there. They established simple shelters for seasonal use on the ridges overlooking their fields but put their dwellings high up on the Chimney Rock cuesta. Such an upland shift among

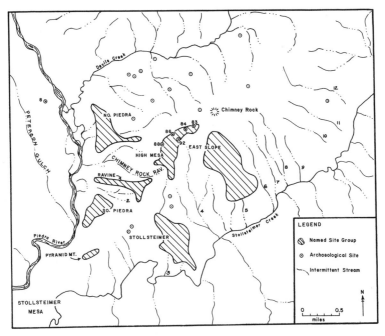

Map of seven village clusters in the Chimney Rock Archeological Area as identified by University of Colorado studies. *After Eddy, 1977, Figure 4.*

Anasazi of this time was not unusual and may hint at regionwide climatic changes, as well as the local problems of population pressures and numbing winter cold trapped in the valleys. Although the rugged terrain suggests a natural defense, there is no concrete sign that physical security was of concern other than a single possible stockade foundation across a trail and several structures strategically placed for traffic control.

The archaeological survey team counted sixteen sites scattered over the mesa wherever the broken ground permitted and crowded along the sheer northern mesa edge leading up to the multiroomed pueblo set against the backdrop of the towering stone pillars. The number of contiguous rooms at any one site was not as great as on the lower north slope. Eddy judged from surface indications that three individual houses, ten structures comprising four multiple units, and seven villages making up a total of ninety-seven rooms were represented.

Many environmental conditions were less favorable here than down below. At 7,400 feet, a slope toward the south did afford a beneficial warming exposure and longer periods of light, but among the drawbacks were more intense storms. Those in summer were accompanied by wicked lightning. There were few substantial patches of land deep enough for cultivation, and a crusty caprock complicated any sort of construction. The major problem to occupation was that there was no immediate source of water other than ephemeral seeps between the Pictured Cliff sandstone and Lewis shale.

The lack of drinking water on the high mesa tested the ingenuity of the Piedrans but was not an insurmountable problem. In winter, snow surely was melted for household use. If the mesa-top structures continued to be occupied in summer, the women and children are assumed to have carried water six hundred to a thousand feet up from the valley floors over rough trails a mile to a mile and a half long. Potters produced large plain gray jars with narrow necks and mouths in which to store this precious resource. Seepage from unglazed earthenwares resulted in considerable liquid loss. The output of such vessels in comparison to those meant for other functions was far greater here than in neighboring Anasazi outposts. Reinforcing the notion of vital storage containers filling every mesa-top home was one study of a very limited sherd lot that seemed to show that the percentage of water jars increased with distance from water sources. Because the vessels themselves were too heavy and cumbersome to carry when full and possibly wet, a different type of receptacle, perhaps tightly woven pitched baskets or skin bags, must have been employed for the actual hauling.

One can envision columns of women and offspring trudging down and up the mesa in an endless replenishment of water and groups of men hiking down to their fields in morning and back to their domiciles at night. It was not uncommon for Anasazi fields to be at some distance from settlements, but in this case the separation between home and farm was more vertical than horizontal. What to modern observers might appear as an overly arduous routine for all family members literally was taken in stride by the Anasazi, for whom life was never easy.

Despite other logistical difficulties, raw materials for building were plentiful on the mesa. The abundant cobblestones on the spurs of land

Eleventh-century small house site (5AA88) on the Chimney Rock mesa after excavation and stabilization. *Courtesy San Juan National Forest.*

next to the river were replaced at greater elevations by outcrops of sandstone. Using heavy stone mauls and hammers, workers broke out rough blocks of this material. Mud and clay for mortar and plaster were present in pockets near house sites, but water with which to prepare them either had to be collected from melting snow in spring or fall or carried up from the rivers at other seasons. A virgin forest yielded ponderosa pine and Douglas fir for primary roofing timbers and piñon and juniper for stringers and insulating layers. The Anasazi felled and prepared them with stone axes or blades, a strenuous task with which they had long experience.

The way in which the stone, earth, and wood were used to create shelters revealed both the persistence of the Piedrans' cultural biases and their adaptability to this high-altitude environment. The three multiple-unit groups excavated by the university diggers showed that the long tradition of round dwellings was ingrained in the Piedran mind-set — they continued to build them on the high mesa. It was as though a house

View of interior living room at Site 5AA88 showing its similarity to older pithouses of the upper San Juan region. *Courtesy University of Colorado.*

was not acceptable unless it was somewhat circular. Ideally, it should also be at least partially subterranean. However, with bedrock so near the surface, the masons could not sink their mesa residences any appreciable depth into the ground. They did install interior features — southern ventilator shaft, fire hearth, four post holes for seating of roof supports, and metate bins — typical of the houses to which they were accustomed. There is no remaining trace of wall plastering. In essence, the Chimney Rock mesa dwellings were pithouses without the pit.

The most unusual characteristics of these rustic edifices were massive, crudely laid masonry walls averaging three feet in thickness. In instances where several round structures were joined, the wall breadth was even greater. Doubtless this kind of wall construction was an adaptation to frigid winters on the exposed, windswept mesa top. To further maintain their customary architectural ideals, the builders attached thick-walled rectangular storage or workrooms on the north or west side of round living rooms, repeating in sandstone what earlier had been made of jacal or cobbles. This continued use into the eleventh

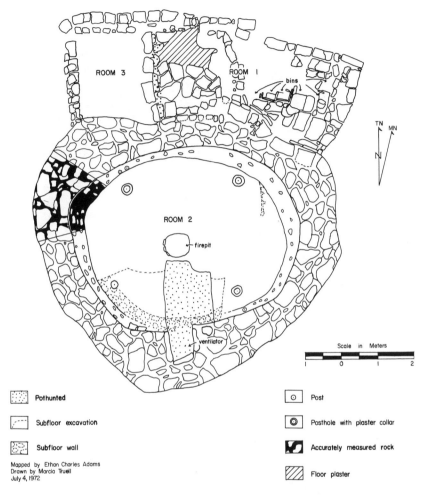

Ground plan of structure at Site 5AA88. Room 2 is partially subterranean; Rooms 1 and 3 are at ground level. *After Eddy, 1977, Figure 29.*

century of the pithouse form and its idiosyncratic appearance makes the architecture of the high-mesa Piedrans and those of contemporaries living along the far eastern peripheries of the Anasazi world distinctive from styles developed in either the Chaco or Mesa Verde areas.

The eleventh-century Piedrans not only favored pithouses, they also had a penchant for putting them on high places. For example, surveyors found two settlements on a sharp pinnacle called Pyramid Mountain, an

A line of milling bins in Room 1 at Site 5AA88 indicates that space was a work area. *Courtesy San Juan National Forest.*

A cache of grinding stones and mauls was recovered in a special-function surface room at Site 5AA88. *Courtesy University of Colorado.*

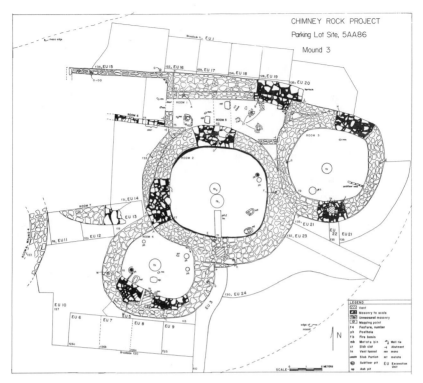

Plan of the Parking Lot Site (5AA86) showing three partially subterranean living rooms flanked on the north by several surface workrooms. *After Eddy, 1977, Figure 25.*

erosional remnant that rises some 250 feet above the southwestern rim of the Chimney Rock mesa. The sides of the peak are steeply sloped, difficult to negotiate, and impossible to cultivate. The area on top of it is so limited and spiny that twelve mounds and pithouse depressions are crammed together as if hanging on. The summit commands an awe-inspiring 360-degree view of the merger of river valleys six hundred feet below with successive tiers of evergreen mountains. Nonetheless, there seems no practical reason to have selected this spot for home sites. Thus, some students regard the Pyramid Mountain group of sites as a ceremonial center, an idea for which there is as yet no supporting evidence.

One excavated structure on Chimney Rock mesa does appear to have served some special function. It was probably both ritualistic and

Parking Lot Site after excavation and stabilization. *Courtesy San Juan National Forest.*

secular in nature and helped to integrate the scattered mesa-top occu-pants into a viable social unit. Eddy called it a "Great Kiva." However, morphologically its relationship to other eastern Anasazi Great Kivas was more that of a second cousin than of a twin. Rather than being substantially below ground level, the Chimney Rock structure was primarily a surficial chamber built on bedrock that sloped southward. Rather than being a true circle in shape, it had a slightly convoluted exterior wall. Rather than having wall niches or encircling rooms for special objects, it featured fourteen rectangular cists sunk into the perimeter of the floor. Rather than being equipped with a bench around the entire circumference, it sported a narrow, finlike projection on the north side of the room that would have served only as a shelf and not as seating for spectators of events going on in the chamber. According to custom, a pair of crudely laid masonry floor vaults was placed on a north-south axis on opposite sides of the kiva. They were irregular in shape but nonetheless vaguely rectangular, as were those known in other districts. Although more semicircular than square, the surviving foun-dation of a central masonry box suggests the usual fireboxes in other

Excavator Frank Eddy stands on a photography ladder at the Parking Lot Site while a helicopter overhead delivers stabilization materials. *Courtesy University of Colorado.*

Great Kivas. Because the stones were not fire-reddened, Eddy preferred to regard the feature as an altar. However, that term ascribes a religious purpose to something others see as strictly utilitarian.

Whether or not the building was roofed is another open question. Little evidence of fallen wooden roof members and just one of the typical four spaced post holes for vertical supports were found. It is possible that the timbers may have been removed at some time for other use. Further, three posts may have rested on bedrock, eliminating the need for seating holes. Although an estimated wall height of less than four feet strength-

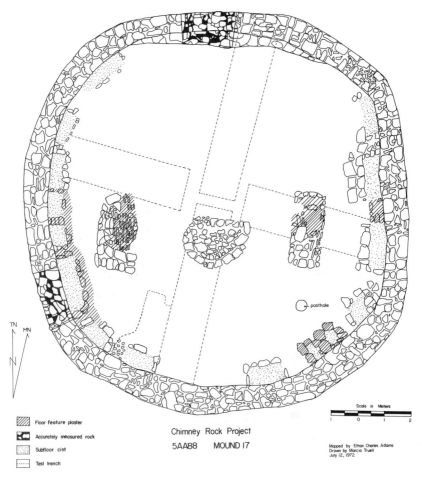

Floor feature plaster
Accurately measured rock
Subfloor cist
Test trench

TN
MN
N

posthole

Scale in Meters
0 1 2

Chimney Rock Project

5AA88   MOUND 17

Mapped by Ethan Charles Adams
Drawn by Marcia Truell
July 12, 1972

Plan of Chimney Rock Great Kiva (Site 5AA88, Mound 17). *After Eddy, 1977, Figure 28.*

ens the no-roof hypothesis, it was obvious to the excavators that much of the superstructure had been removed prehistorically. In view of the prevailing lack of architectural refinement seen in the Piedran struc-tures, it might well have been beyond the builders' capabilities to span the more than forty-foot diameter of this structure. A partial roof was an alternative. However, an exposed chamber collecting snow from October to June and filling with rainwater in summer could have been of little use. Contributing to the mystery of this building is the matter

Great Kiva after 1971–1972 excavation. Note roots of large trees that had grown over the wall of the abandoned structure. *Courtesy University of Colorado.*

Great Kiva on Chimney Rock mesa after stabilization. One floor vault is at right. Rocks in the center may have been a collapsed firebox. A partial narrow bench runs along the north wall; opened floor pits are at right. A small house (Site 5AA88) is visible at center rear. *Courtesy San Juan National Forest.*

of how it was entered. The usual surface antechamber and stairs leading down into a subsurface room were absent, suggesting either that there was no roof or that there was a roof hatchway. Although an awkward way to get into such a large surface building, to Piedrans accustomed to hatchway entrances to their above-ground pithouses it would have seemed a logical solution. Was the whole structure a botched job, or were the Piedrans simply doing their own thing?

The portable artifacts taken from the structure were the usual stone implements — axes, choppers, and gravers. Fragments of plain gray earthenware jars were present. No ceremonial goods were found, but that does not necessarily indicate a strictly social usage of the building. Four small rectangular earthenware blocks with holes, in which it has been suggested feathers could be inserted, were found in the nearby dwelling and may have been part of ritual accoutrements used in the large chamber. Some relationship between the two neighboring buildings is possible.

Tree-ring analysis of wood specimens from the multiroomed domestic structure indicates that trees needed for construction were cut during summer months. Generally, Anasazi farmers at lower elevations reserved this activity for periods of the year when crops did not need tending. Eddy suggests a time of plentiful rainfall that allowed farmers the freedom to do other tasks. Planks for the kiva floor cists were cut from summer-harvested wood. The range of tree-ring dates for the cist planks is from A.D. 994 to 1084. The early date likely came from a piece of old downed wood that was picked up and put to use. The latter may have come from a replacement for a worn specimen. Of twelve dates, one-third were in the 1070s. That period seems a probable construction time for the large building. Although there was an earlier occupation at the nearby house, the 1070s also represented an active building episode there.

With this one obviously specialized structure verified through excavation, it is possible that other large depressions on the lower terraces, some up to seventy feet in diameter, contain similar remains. From Piedra Phase times, villages on the San Juan usually included one oversized pithouse that most regional archaeologists interpret as a community center. The concept of such a building likely was carried up the Piedra. However, the number of large depressions in the environs of

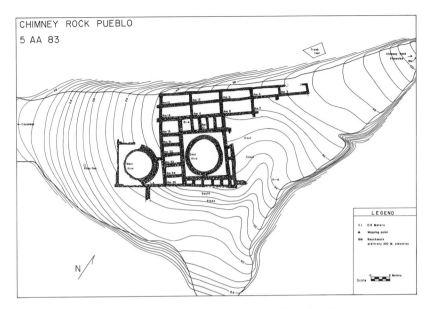

Plan of the excavated portions of the Chimney Rock pueblo (Site 5AA83).
After Eddy, 1977, Figure 12.

Chimney Rock (Eddy cites thirty-six) is too great for the normal ratio of Great Kivas to domiciles. Could it be that the insularity of the upper Piedrans gave rise to a religious intensification requiring more special places in which to perform rituals? Recovered materials do not reflect such an elaboration. Nor are there small kivas for more intimate ceremonies such as typify other Anasazi villages.

As the eleventh century drew to a close and after long periods of virtual isolation from the rest of the Anasazi world, a thunderbolt of outside influence hit the Chimney Rock mesa. This influence was expressed in the large pueblo on the caprock of the most prominent 7,600-foot level of the cuesta, from where it dominated the lower indigenous settlements. Jeancon's judgment in 1921 that it was reflective of the architectural style of Chaco Canyon was reaffirmed in 1970, when the university crew removed fallen debris and carried out limited excavation. What was exposed was the ruin of an edificial form known in Chaco studies as a Great House. It was a planned, multistory roomblock of core and veneer sandstone masonry, with large, high-ceilinged rooms and incorporated dual kivas, one of which was of a Chacoan style. It was totally unlike any other architectural complex on the Piedra.

At the time of Jeancon's work, the Chimney Rock pueblo was only the second such Chacoan structure excavated outside Chaco Canyon itself. The first was at Aztec Ruins in New Mexico forty miles southwest of Chimney Rock. The relationships of these sites to broader Chaco regional developments were not explored at the time the remains were originally studied. Only after another half-century of research would it be realized that these two sites were part of a network of similar structures that stretched out in all directions from the hub of Chaco Canyon, in some cases as far as several hundred miles. Now known as "outliers," these structures are regarded as manifestations of a burst of efflorescence. During a period of about seventy-five years straddling the eleventh and twelfth centuries, Anasazi culture in bleak, resource-deficient Chaco Canyon came to an amazing climax called the Chaco Phenomenon. The number of identified Great Houses is now in excess of seventy-five, with more being found yearly. Not only were the edifices built according to a more-or-less standardized model, but the entire outlier system was organized. Commonly, Great Houses were built within a dense settlement, situated on a prominence, spaced approximately seventeen miles apart, and occasionally in late times positioned on a roadway. Frequently, a Great Kiva was also in the locality. The relationship of all these Great Houses to each other remains unknown.

The Chimney Rock Great House varied from this format. It stood at one side of the indigenous high mesa community, removed from the aggregates of dwellings rather than in the center of occupation. Topography probably dictated this placement. As indicated, the large, specialized chamber farther down the mesa top does not fit the Great Kiva stereotype and seems to date from as much as fifteen to twenty years earlier. As yet, no Great House has been documented in the intervening region between Chimney Rock and its nearest Chacoan neighbor, Aztec Ruins, making the distance between them more than twice the usual amount for outliers. Nor has a prehistoric road been noted in the vicinity. Roberts's chance discovery closer to the San Juan of a small basin cut into bedrock and a possible signaling station, both features commonly associated with the Chacoan sphere, lead one to suspect that somewhere

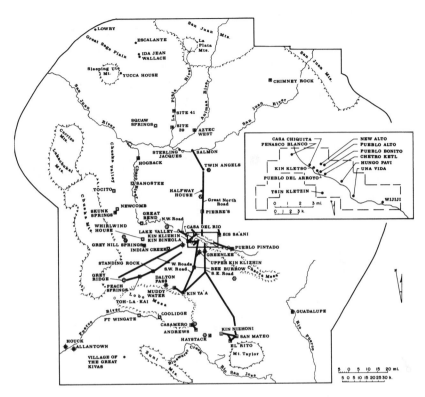

Known system of prehistoric Chaco roads does not reach as far north as Chimney Rock. *After Powers, Gillespie, and Lekson, 1983, Figure 1.*

in the unexplored lands south of Chimney Rock another Great House eventually may be found.

Aside from preparing the way for public visitation at the Chimney Rock Great House, the university researchers sought wood samples from which to obtain the dates that Jeancon was unable to provide. They were successful in this effort but prompted a controversy that remains unresolved. One cross pole from the ventilator shaft of the lower east kiva produced a tree-ring date of A.D. 1076. Eddy accepts that date as the time of the building of the kiva and, by extension, the remainder of the roomblock. However, colleagues suspect that the wood specimen probably was a reused timber salvaged from one of the structures on the lower mesa. Supporting this idea is the fact that of fifty-three dates

Archaeologists wrapping tree-ring specimens from Room 8 of the Chimney Rock pueblo, some of which yielded a probable cutting date of A.D. 1093. *Courtesy University of Colorado.*

obtained from wood samples recovered in the local small sites, twenty-six are in the 1070s, whereas only two of the forty-seven specimens reclaimed from the Great House are of that decade. Consequently, these researchers believe the Great House construction was accomplished in one short-term effort in the 1090s. Twenty-six samples of the fallen ceiling wood from one room securely date to 1093, and five eroded samples from the rebuilt east kiva also likely were cut in that year. Eddy proposes that a second remodeling of the site took place then to repair or change what was done in 1076. However, the east kiva and other sectors of the houseblock actually could have been redone while general construction was still underway, perhaps to correct miscalculations in planning, rather than seventeen years after initial construction.

If this revised dating interpretation is correct, the Great House erection postdated known construction in the indigenous community by a decade and a half or more. The most recent date from the local structures is the 1084 Great Kiva cist plank, which may not reflect time of building. That is not to say that the local populace was gone. A partially burned branch taken from a domestic firepit in an indigenous house dates to 1087, and proposed dates for pollen from the fill of another hearth range from 1090 to 1100. The 1090s also witnessed intense building efforts within Chaco Canyon, as well as outlier construction elsewhere north of the San Juan River, including that at the Salmon and Lowry ruins.

The enigma of the Chimney Rock Great House begins with the identity of its builders. Its style and the degree of craftsmanship exhibited in most of its construction suggest that a cadre of Chaco masons migrated northward to do the job. Were they conquerors, colonists, or neither? There is no indication that the intrusion was accompanied by force. If they were colonists, traders, or missionaries, how did they communicate with the local people? Some linguists now think the Chacoans spoke Keresan and the Piedrans spoke Tewa. Others believe all people in the northern San Juan spoke Tewa. The best farm plots surely had been worked for generations by the Piedrans; did the Chacoans, because they had more power or more experience with water control and other agricultural methods, simply take these plots? Or did they impose some sort of tribute in the form of goods or foodstuffs? Did they regard the Piedrans as country bumpkins who were not even able to build a proper Great Kiva? Provocative as these questions are, it is improbable that the outliers were the product of companies of male colonists who permanently left their womenfolk at home. One theory, noting the large number of outliers and the number of them being erected at the same time, has specialized construction crews being dispatched from Chaco Canyon to carry out the various building projects. This work may have been done in return for services or products from the local populace. It is also possible that the Chaco influence was so pervasive across the entire eastern Colorado Plateau by the close of the eleventh century that local workers became willing apprentices under the guidance of a Cha-coan *mayordomo*. The fact that the western portion of the houseblock was less well constructed and the associated kiva lacked usual Chacoan characteristics may reflect indigenous workmanship.

A diluted Chaco style of masonry was noted by Roberts in 1922 in one small house the State Historical and Natural History Society crew dug on a lower terrace. Some pottery and bits of turquoise taken from its fill dirt likewise pointed to a Chaco connection. This site, and perhaps others as yet unexcavated, could have resulted either from a direct intrusion of Chacoans or, more likely, some locals strongly under the Chaco spell.

Regardless of who was responsible for building the Chimney Rock Great House, the task was a formidable one. Just what was the motivat-ing force behind its presence in a backward community with little prior association with Chacoans and on a piece of property that seemingly presented no practical advantage? The selection of that location and the sheer difficulty of building there can be seen as symbolizing authority, which leads to the explanation for the outlier system. Many scholars now believe that it was devised and administered by a Chacoan elite as a means of bringing a continual supply of required resources into the core area of Chaco Canyon or redistributing them to satellites in return for some sort of sociopolitical, economic, or religious patronage, if not actual goods. The primary resource the upper Piedra district could have provided under such a scheme was timber used in Chaco Canyon, where there were almost no trees yet where hundreds of thousands of logs were utilized. The Chimney Rock cuesta may have been especially attractive because ponderosa pines were available on the lower slopes. Archaeolo-gist Allan Kane would have the men controlling this traffic living in the Chimney Rock Great House, postulating the simpler structures down the mesa as the lumberjacks' camps and those on the bluffs nearer the river as the point at which crews actually floated logs downriver to some point such as Salmon Ruin, from where they could have been trans-ported via a road into Chaco. This is a fascinating but as yet unverifiable plot. Studies of trace elements in wood recovered at Chaco eventually may pin down a number of sources, the slopes of the Chuskas to the west of Chaco among them. The low frequency in the Chimney Rock assemblages of stone tools that could have been used in logging discounts the notion of such specialized activity. Also, even though some timber may well have been taken from the Chimney Rock district, why put the command post on top of a thousand-foot-high mesa, where there was nothing more than a view? How were simple farmers, whose preceding dozen generations had laboriously tilled the terraces, converted into virtual chain gangs of wholesale woodsmen? Would they have accepted such interference with their traditional round of summer duties? And what did the locals get in return? Apparently not material things: virtually nothing came from the excavators' trenches that could be identified as diagnostically Chacoan other than a handful of potsherds and several tiny flakes of turquoise. The lack of classic Chaco pottery can be explained in part by its very restricted distribution away from the canyon proper and the wholesale switch in the early twelfth century across the northern San Juan Basin to a vegetal-painted McElmo style.

What some scholars believe the Piedrans did get from an inflow of Chaco power was a recharging of religious batteries. One school of thought has the Great House edging up to the feet of the sacred stony Twin War Gods in order to bask in their aura and draw strength or protection. For some 250 years the Piedrans lived with these anthropo-morphized pillars on the eastern horizon, and, if present custom gives any indication, felt their supernatural energy and perhaps appeased them with offerings or prayers. Why at the end of the eleventh century should they feel compelled to move closer? Maybe because of some Chacoan drive toward greater concern for help from their gods.

Another school argues that the houseblock was built as a watch-tower from which to observe astronomical phenomena having great importance in regulating the ceremonial calendar, which in turn was bound up with the yearly cycle of planting and harvesting. An accurate calendar would have been of utmost importance to a group in a marginal agricultural setting, where a few weeks too early or too late in planting could have been disastrous for crops. Although most identified celestial features among Anasazi remains have to do with the sun, from whom the Twin War Gods descended, astronomer McKim Malville points out a sequence of lunar events that might have been watched during the second half of the eleventh century by Chimney Rock residents. The moon has symbolic life and death meaning for the Pueblo Indians of today, and its monthly cycle segments the year. Malville's computer-determined phenomena include full moons rising between the pinnacles near the time of three winter solstices, a particularly significant time for modern Pueblo Indians, or another three periods called lunar standstills, when the moon has reached sufficiently high northern declination to appear between the columns as many as forty times per period. Malville ties these lunar events to the two tree-ring dates of 1076 and 1093 obtained from the Great House. He suggests that observations around 1076 prompted refurbishing of the Great House at the later date in order to create a more adequate viewing place. However, he fails to note that there is no information available about the exact form of the upper walls of the edifice or whether they would have improved viewing opportunities.

Over the years, the Piedrans were on hand to take note of the standstill periods, fourteen or fifteen of which occurred before June 1094, and the more frequent correspondence of full moon and winter solstices. Even though the view from the lower mesa might have been obscured because of the lay of the land or less dramatic than the view from higher up, and even though it would not have had the pinnacles as an immediate foresight, quite surely the Piedrans observed these celestial dramas with keen interest. Moreover, Malville's team determined that an indigenous house structure on the highlands west of the Piedra River and a supposed tower on the Chimney Rock mesa were in the necessary alignment with the two chimneys to serve as places from which sun watchers could have made calculations relative to the solar solstices. The alleged tower happened to be situated in the side of a swale that might have hampered observations, and its upper construction is unknown. Whether or not such site locations were coincidental will never be known for sure. But would prior interest in sunrises silhouetting the stone columns and moonrises shining through the space between them have prompted the Piedrans to help the Chacoans raise the large building crowning the mesa? Perhaps yes, if they were overwhelmed by a desire to share in whatever magic it was that the Chacoans briefly exerted over their fellow eastern Anasazi. In Malville's view, the Cha-

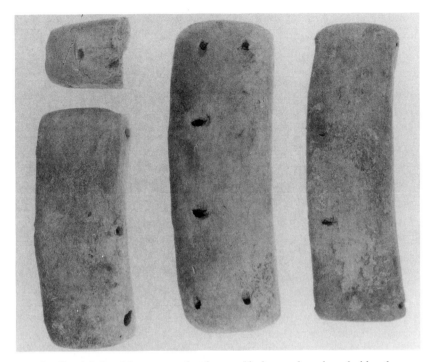

Small, solid clay slabs punctured with spaced holes may have been holders for sacred feather plumes. In addition to eleven specimens reclaimed from Chimney Rock settlements, others have been found in prehistoric remains in Chaco Canyon and appear to have been used in modern times in Hopi ceremonies. *Courtesy Marcia Truell Newren.*

coans were so astronomically sophisticated they would have exploited for their own ends a local knowledge of these lunar phenomena. To him, the guardhouse, the tiny building spanning the narrow ridge of land leading up to the Great House (excavated for a third time in 1988), was meant to control traffic into a sacred precinct dedicated to astronomical purposes. If that were in fact the reason for the Chimney Rock Great House, it would be the only outlier thus far linked specifically to religion.

The Chimney Rock Great House itself was not any sort of specialized ceremonial edifice, nor did it need architects trained in skills restricted to a religious elite that may or may not have been attuned to what was taking place in the sky. Albeit of more refined construction than most, in many respects the Great House was just like scores of other roomblocks found from southwestern Colorado to the Little Colorado drainage of west central New Mexico and eastern Arizona. It may have been meant as nonresidential public architecture, even though it was partly occupied: if the motivation for its establishment was ritualistic in nature, it may have been a center to which periodic pilgrimages were directed. However, there is no known road along which the faithful may have traveled nor is there sufficient residue of material things to confirm large-scale gatherings or feasting.

The one category of goods recovered that might conceivably be interpreted as ceremonial are eleven so-called feather holders, only several of which were found in the large pueblo. One came from the fill of the east kiva. Technical analyses of the clays from which they were formed indicate five different unidentified sources. Perhaps feather holders made at a number of places were carried to Chimney Rock for special rites. Several have been found in Chaco.

Whatever the reasons for putting the Chimney Rock Great House where it is, the adventure was short-lived. After only two further lunar standstills and the cutting of several thousand logs, it was all over. Beginning about A.D. 1130–1135, the great design evolved at Chaco Canyon started to collapse, taking many of the outliers, probably including that at Chimney Rock, with it. In the wake of failure, neither astronomical observations nor procurement of resources was important. Some outliers were reoccupied by Mesa Verdeans after the twelfth-century Chaco abandonment, but Chimney Rock was not among them.

Another of the many unanswered questions concerning Chimney Rock is whether the Piedrans themselves may have led the exodus from the area. If so, the absence of a local support group could have hastened the demise of the outlier as a cog in the Chaco system. Conversely, without the presumed unifying force of the Chaco Phenomenon, the indigenous population may have been more vulnerable to debilitating circumstances. One of these was another dry cycle that gripped the upper San Juan district as the Great House construction began. It eased for a time early in the twelfth century, only to become very severe after 1130. If they had not already departed, that prolonged drought surely would have prompted the Piedra Anasazi to move on. After they left, the

Chimney Rock district would never again be home to as many individuals as it had been during their tenure.

When the Piedrans did leave the mesa, it was not just a matter of their going to another terrace several miles upriver. This time they moved off the Colorado Plateau. Did they look back and ponder the trauma of leaving the Twin War Gods? Or if they took comfort in the presence of these deities, did they feel betrayed when things turned sour?

A route proposed by scholars would have taken the Piedrans south along the San Juan River to where Largo and Gobernador canyons opened to the east. As the migrants went up these pathways toward the Continental Divide, they were among peoples sharing a similar cultural base. A familiar variety of architecture and settlement patterns and a comparable array of portable material things eased their way. By the end of the twelfth century, the Piedrans are thought to have reached the Gallina uplands in New Mexico, northwest of modern Jemez Pueblo. It was an environment in which they were comfortable, one of high mesas dissected by canyons in a transition zone between ponderosa pine and juniper. Architectural and artifactual evidence confirms that they settled there for about another century, after which they disappeared from the cultural record.

Several elders of Taos Pueblo, the northernmost of the modern Pueblo Indian villages, claim that one of their clans originated at the Chimney Rock communities. To date, there is no archaeological confirmation of this legend in any direct line between the two localities. The long passage covering several centuries from the foot of the San Juan Mountains to the foot of the Sangre de Cristo Mountains may have looped southward through the Gallina district.

Back at Chimney Rock, the empty houses fell into ruin. Many roofs burned. Perhaps they were ignited by departing occupants. Perhaps lightning struck them or nearby trees, setting them ablaze. The charred or rotted timbers sank inward into the above-ground pithouses, leaving the landscape scarred with man-made craters. The great paired pinnacles topping the cuesta were enveloped in a deep silence that remained unbroken for nearly half a millennium.

PART III

EPILOGUE

5

THE CHIMNEY ROCK DISTRICT TO 1900

In the fall of 1626 a group of Capote Utes walked several hundred miles out of their customary hunting grounds in the San Juan Mountains to Jemez. They established a camp close by. On this occasion their purpose was to trade hides, dried meat, and berries for salt, textiles, and foodstuffs raised by the Pueblo Indian farmers. In other winters their southerly migrations to the vicinity of the northwesternmost Spanish settlement of Abiquiu typically were to escape from severe cold. When spring arrived at Jemez, the Capotes again packed up and traveled back along the Chama River to the foot of the craggy mountains and then northwest into the recesses of what is now southern Colorado. They very likely paused for a time to enjoy the waters of a large, bubbling thermal spring at a bend in the San Juan River just twenty miles east of Chimney Rock and Companion Rock. Periodic long-term interactions such as this one between the nomadic mountain tribes and the sedentary villagers of the Rio Grande probably was an established pattern, but in 1626 it was noted by Spanish scribes at Santa Fe for the first time. The Capote Utes had come out from the shadows of the rocks and briefly entered documented history, only to soon disappear back into their lofty wilderness.

Three of the seven distinct bands of Utes occupied a large swath of land along the northern flanks of the Spanish holdings in New Mexico. The Capotes claimed the territory from the headwaters of the San Juan River west to the upper Animas River, including a huge slice of the mountains buttressing the north side of this region. On further west toward what is now the Four Corners were the Wiminuches. East of the

Capotes in the San Luis Valley and along the eastern slopes of the Rockies and bordering plains were the Moaches.

Exactly where and when the Utes originated as a tribe remains unclear. Being constantly on the move in search of game and edible plants and having only meager worldly goods, they left little imprint upon the land for archaeologists to study. It is generally believed, however, that sometime between the fifteenth and sixteenth centuries they drifted down through the great western intermontane basin, gradually spreading through 150,000 square miles of semiarid eastern Utah, western Colorado, and into the Rocky Mountains. The fact that they spoke a Shoshonean language similar to that of the Hopis of north central Arizona, the Paiutes of southern Utah, and the Comanches of the southern plains suggests a remote common ancestry.

Prehistoric Ute occupation in this vast area has been noted by the occasional residue of brush huts, game traps, rock art, and a few small objects used in food gathering and processing. The latter include chipped projectile points, stone choppers, handstones, and milling slabs, tatters of baskets or cordage, and rare, poorly made earthenware jars. Generally speaking, the Utes shared an impoverished Desert Culture that had been typical of other Great Basin groups for several thousand years. That is what they likely carried as cultural attributes whenever they arrived in the Chimney Rock district.

But then a fundamental change took place because the temptation to own Spanish horses proved irresistible. By the 1640s the Southern Utes were the first western tribe to be mounted after stealing or trading for animals from neighboring Spanish *rancherías* and pastures. Learning to skillfully handle and breed the stock changed their character. No longer were they shy primitives hiding behind the peaks. Emboldened with new self-confidence, they traveled far and wide. This mobility brought them for the first time into significant association with surrounding Native Americans and with Europeans. Both offered advantages and posed threats.

The Southern Utes seem to have been most influenced by their linguistic relatives, the Comanches. Because the Moaches were geographically closest to these people, they served as agents in introducing some aspects of borrowed Plains culture to other Utes. Leather leggings and untailored outer garments were adopted. Interest in quill-, feather-, and beadwork grew accordingly. Skin-covered tepees replaced the brush wickiups erected earlier. Although the Comanches and the Moache Utes enjoyed a friendly alliance during the years when both were becoming increasingly aggressive and wide-ranging and both relied at times on help from the Jicarilla Apaches, the relationships eventually broke down, with repeated casualties on all sides.

Throughout the seventeenth century there were conflicts between Spaniards and Utes. The primary band involved appears to have been the Moaches, whose range overlapped that of the northern probings of the Spanish realm. Territorial rights were at stake. The Capotes remained secure in a region still unexplored by Europeans but periodically came into Spanish communities to trade hides, buffalo robes, and slaves for metal tools, beads, and the fine blankets made by the Pueblos. Such intercourse hastened an acculturation that was slow in coming to the Capotes because of their remoteness. In 1670 the Spaniards signed a treaty with the Southern Ute bands, and none are thought to have joined the revolt spearheaded by the Pueblos that ten years later drove the hated white masters out of New Mexico for a twelve-year period.

That uprising did directly affect the Capotes, however. At the end of the seventeenth century some Navajos and residents of Jemez banded together to move into Capote territory in order to escape probable Spanish reprisals against them. At the time, the San Juan River was considered a natural, if highly permeable, border between Navajos and Capote and Wiminuche Utes. One of the earliest Spanish explorers into the district recognized this fact when he noted, "This stream [San Juan River] is called the Rio Grande del Navajo because it separates the province of this name from the Yuta nation" (Motter 1984, 25).

Prehistorically, Navajos in some number lived along most of the northern tributaries of the San Juan, although many more concentrated in the broken tablelands drained by the Largo and Gobernador rivers to the south. That was the homeland they now know as the Dinetah. Whether the Piedra River valley was one of those utilized by Navajos prior to 1700 remains a question for future research. If so, it is possible that incoming Utes routed them out for a time.

As with the Utes, nothing about the Navajos or their cultural heritage prior to their appearance in the Southwest is known. The point of origination of Athabaskan-speaking Apachean bands, which include the Navajos, is suggested to have been in the Mackenzie Basin of Canada. In the course of many centuries, they made their way south, reaching the northern Colorado Plateau some time after the departure of the Anasazi and before the arrival of the Utes along the region's northern perimeters. Recent archaeology puts them in the La Plata drainage of southwestern Colorado by the mid-1400s. The first Spanish reference to the Navajos places them in the greater Southwest at the time of Coronado's 1540 *entrada*. Early Navajo social or ceremonial organization is unstudied, but this group differed from its Apache relatives in engaging in rudimentary farming to supplement a basic hunting and gathering subsistence. That lifestyle required seasonal sedentism, which is substantiated by occasional finds of remains of their shelters. These were created by upright logs arranged in a tight circle and interlocked at their tops to form a conical frame, and the whole was made secure by a covering of earth, brush, and stones. A rough utilitarian kind of pottery, quite distinctive from that made by the Pueblos, is found associated with these structures. Also recovered are simple stone implements used in hunting and in food preparation.

The mixed group of peoples who took refuge in Capote territory following the Spanish reconquest of New Mexico in 1692 appears to have preferred the more open valleys to the west of the Piedra, which afforded better horticultural possibilities. However, this impression may result from lack of archaeology along the central section of the Piedra rather than absence of relevant sites there. A limited refugee occupation did occur at the now submerged confluence of the San Juan and Piedra rivers, and a scattering of seventeenth-century Pueblo potsherds has been recorded within sight of the Chimney Rock–Companion Rock pinnacles.

There is not as much evidence north of the San Juan of the cultural transfusion that occurred elsewhere, wherein Navajo culture was re-vamped according to the Pueblo model. Nor is there the assortment of Spanish goods — bullet casings, metal axes and hammers, pieces of glazed earthenware, sheep bones — that might have come into Navajo

Remains of an eighteenth-century Navajo forked-stick hogan in the Navajo Reservoir district (Site LA 4071). *Courtesy Museum of New Mexico.*

hands through the Pueblos. This absence of evidence reflects the fact that the refugee influx north of the San Juan was an overflow from the Dinetah and probably involved only a few hundred Navajos and a handful of Pueblos who were geographically separated from the central zone of contact. The upper San Juan was a cultural backwater then as it had been when the Anasazi were around. Its most obvious remains of the refugee period are the usual Navajo forked-stick hogans, *ramadas*, fire hearths, storage pits, and camps in rock overhangs. Only infrequently are these structures situated near the small cellular masonry rooms in defensive locations believed to have been used by the Pueblo contingent. Any significant impact on Navajo house style by the Pueblos is lacking. However, rock art scratched or painted on cliff faces suggests a notable elaboration of Navajo costume and ritual attributable to Pueblo influence. Pottery of typical tapered-bottom Navajo forms but bearing painted decoration; holes in houses' dirt floors to support looms; clay spindle whorls; wooden prayer sticks and bull roarers; stone bird fetishes; and other lesser objects are further indications of an upgrading

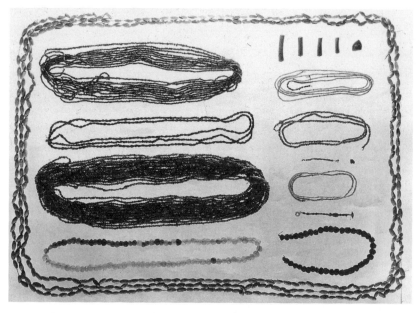

Metal crosses bearing figures of the Savior and the Virgin, metal buttons, buckle, horse gear, and many feet of variously colored glass beads were left behind in structures south of the San Juan River occupied by Pueblo Indians fleeing Spanish reprisals after the revolt of 1680–1692. *Courtesy University of Colorado Museum, Earl Morris Collection.*

Early eighteenth-century Pueblo refugee structure on the Gobernador drainage of New Mexico south of the San Juan River. *Courtesy University of Colorado Museum, Earl Morris Collection.*

of Navajo culture as a result of the years of cohabitation. Moreover, Pueblo influence flowed to the Navajos from the distant past. These early Navajos may not yet have acquired an ingrained fear of the spirits of the dead — they rifled some of the many ancient Pueblo antiquities to be found along the main and side channels of the upper San Juan, reclaiming stone and bone implements that had been discarded hundreds of years earlier. They also converted Anasazi burial chambers into storage places.

The Capotes tolerated the intruders for about fifty years. At the end of that time, the small Pueblo population either had been absorbed by the larger Navajo community or had returned to its traditional home. At mid-eighteenth century, resentful over unwanted competition for resources, the Utes rose up and drove the Navajos back south of the San Juan River. For the next hundred years the Capotes continued to regard the Navajos as their enemies. On occasion they went as far south as

Mount Taylor or southwest to Canyon de Chelly to attack the Navajos on their own ground. This enmity eventually peaked in the 1860s when U.S. troops employed Ute scouts to track down Navajos for incarceration at Fort Sumner.

The aggression against Navajos was just one expression of warlike attitudes on the part of the Capotes. As strong, mounted nomads worldwide have done, they took advantage of more peaceful, earthbound farmers. During the late seventeenth and throughout the eighteenth century, the Capotes preyed upon the sedentary agricultural Hopis, swooping out of their mountain fastness and riding pell-mell across the barren wastes of the San Juan Basin, lured westward by granaries full of corn and beans. Then they turned on the Spaniards of the lower Chama River valley. The Utes left the unprotected mud villages of Abiquiu, Ojo Caliente, and Embudo in ruins. By 1747 Spanish authorities had endured enough. They launched a counteroffensive, only to learn firsthand that the Capotes had an advantage: a haven hostile to unknowledgeable outsiders.

For the 150 years that New Mexico had been a province of the Spanish Crown, the area beyond the high mountains ringing the western San Luis Valley of southern Colorado, the hunting grounds of the Capotes, remained unknown to Europeans. The first non-Indian party believed to have penetrated this pristine domain was that of Juan María Rivera, who in 1765 crossed into the San Juan Mountains and lived to tell of his travels. Eleven years later friars Domínguez and Escalante, on their unsuccessful journey to map a route from Santa Fe to San Francisco, worked down along the terraces hemming in the San Juan River. One of its northern tributaries they knew as the *Río de la Piedra Parada,* named for a pair of towering stone columns seen far away against the skyline of this drainage. Whether they or an earlier unidentified party actually first applied this name is uncertain. Eager to move westward, Domínguez and Escalante did not venture up the stream but were the first to make written mention of its dominating natural monuments. None of these initial *entradas* had any significant effect upon the natives of the district.

Once it was shown to be possible to go and come safely through this uncharted world of extreme topography and unknown numbers of Ute savages, an adventurous few Spaniards back on the Rio Grande were eager to establish trade relations with the Indians. In earlier times it was the Utes themselves who had initiated an active exchange of supple deer and elk hides processed by Capote women for desired woolen goods, beads, and utensils. Winter after winter as they pitched their tepees in the Chama Valley bottom below Abiquiu, some of the band went further downriver to trade with residents of San Juan and Santa Clara pueblos or to walk the streets of Santa Fe quietly waiting for Spanish customers. However, in the late eighteenth century, in order to promote a greater volume of exchange, the Spanish colonial government began licensing individuals to take their commodities directly to nomadic Indians circling the fringes of European civilization. Some unscrupulous men hastened to exploit this opening and dealt in contraband whiskey and guns. Whether legitimate or not, this frontier commerce yielded an important benefit to the administration: a growing knowledge of the northwestern outlands.

As the Mexican administration took over New Mexico in the early 1800s, the Chimney Rock district of southern Colorado was rapidly being opened up. A number of trails used by itinerant traders out of the Rio Grande Valley already snaked through what had been virgin Capote range. Paths along the watercourses were tramped down by a rag-tag assemblage of beaver trappers, horse thieves, fur traders, and mountain men headquartered at Taos. English names dotting contemporary accounts indicate they were largely from the United States. In 1829 a 1,200-mile-long mule track, grandly termed the Old Spanish Trail (although the Spaniards never had traversed it), was blazed from Santa Fe to Los Angeles. Its first sectors followed a Capote route from Abiquiu north up the Chama River, across some of the highlands where Navajo and Pueblo refugees once had hidden, then across the San Juan River at its junction with the Piedra, before taking off for the arid mesa country of Utah. It was in active use during the 1830s and 1840s by muleteers driving annual caravans laden with bundles of Pueblo blankets from New Mexico to California and returning with strings of hundreds of horses and mules. The Capotes, many then camped along the lower Piedra under the leadership of a man named Tamuche, resigned themselves to the movement of this foreign traffic through their southern territory. Meanwhile, Mexican settlers, who posed a more enduring threat, were closing in. The broad San Luis Valley north of Taos attracted some; Moache warriors burned them out. North of Abiquiu, the Tierra Amarilla land grant finalized in 1832 brought Hispanos to the verdant foothills of the San Juan Mountains, which the Capotes regarded as theirs. Despite their reputation for settling scores without much provocation, the Capotes observed an amazing few years of peace in the upper San Juan–Chama region. With the United States standing at the gates, that was soon to change.

The decade of the 1850s was a time of travail for all Native Americans in the northern Southwest, even more so for the newly installed U.S. territorial government. It had to maintain order across a piece of the continent it scarcely knew, populated with peoples of many backgrounds it did not understand. One of the first moves it made was to secure a treaty with Capote and Moache elders. Their hungry followers had taken to raiding Mexican farms of the upper Chama area because of threatened starvation. Hunting activities by Hispanos and other whites encroaching upon tribal lands had decimated or driven away much of the wildlife upon which the Indians depended. Kit Carson, newly appointed U.S. Indian agent, estimated that there were then between eight and nine thousand Capotes. Under treaty terms, he was responsible for issuing them rations out of a hastily established depot set up at Abiquiu. Soon a second treaty was negotiated, with stipulations that in return for dole the Capotes would try farming. To agriculturally oriented Americans, that seemed the surest alternative to depending for survival upon the providence of an uncontrolled nature. To the Utes, whose hunting and gathering tradition was millennia long, it was unthinkable. Dole continued; farming never commenced.

U.S. penetration into the heart of Capote territory began in 1859, when an army party headed by Capt. John N. Macomb of the Corps of Topographical Engineers set out to retrace the Old Spanish Trail into Utah. The men went from Abiquiu, the jumping-off place for northern explorations, to the San Juan River near the Navajo River confluence, then to the well-known thermal springs at the bend of the San Juan below Wolf Creek Pass. Macomb called the springs Pagosa, a Ute word meaning "boiling water." Later promotion brochures proclaimed it "the largest, hottest spring in the world." From there the party proceeded west along the foothills of the San Juan Mountains, creating a path still used in the present — now it is designated U.S. Highway 160. The men camped one night on a stream they named the Nutria (Spanish word meaning "otter") and the following day wound around the sheer north side of the Chimney Rock cuesta to make a ford of the upper Piedra River. The imposing Chimney Rock formation was sketched by geologist John Newberry. Later, artist J. J. Young produced a lithograph from Newberry's drawing but greatly exaggerated the space between the chimneys. Newberry, who wrote detailed descriptions of other prehistoric remains seen during the survey, failed to note those on the headlands of the Piedra. Newberry did comment upon a Capote encampment the men passed twelve miles west of Pagosa Springs, where women were busy collecting and drying berries and cleaning and dressing hides. Other Ute camps were seen on the Piedra and Pine terraces. Perhaps one was on Stollsteimer Mesa, where Roberts in 1923 reported finding tepee poles and rings and a scattering of glass beads.

The future was crashing in upon the Southern Utes in the early 1860s. It began when Charles Baker discovered gold in the highest San Juans, sparking the growth of the nearby boom camp of Silverton. A more inaccessible spot could hardly be imagined. Range after range of the continent's most rugged mountains blocked a direct route from the towns just getting established along eastern Colorado foothills. Baker saw that the best negotiable gateway for the throng he anticipated would soon come to cash in on his strike was a route long familiar to the Utes. It ran along the broad valley east of the mountainous blockade of the San Juans, around its southern tip, to the avenue leading north provided by the Chama drainage. A man of enterprise, Baker carved out a wagon road from Abiquiu to Pagosa and on to Devil Creek behind the Chimney Rock battlement, built the first bridges across the Piedra and Pine, and then made a rocky trail beside the gushing Animas up to his mining camp. The route was formally chartered by the first Colorado state legislature on January 16, 1877, to be known as the Animas City, Pagosa Springs, and Conejos Wagon Road. Rates were set at one dollar for each vehicle and span of horses. Baker staked out housesites at the thermal springs to sell to those who might not want to endure frigid winters at

10,000 feet. The wilderness was to be tamed, at tremendous cost to those who had been there first and preferred to have it remain as it was.

The Capotes were then living in the Chama area, raising a few goats and existing off government rations, but they did not take kindly to the developments going on in other parts of their territory. They so frequently attacked men bound for the Animas gold fields that the government was forced to prohibit prospectors from entering the San Juans. Nevertheless, the lure of gold outweighed risks and illegalities, and the traffic continued. What appeared to be a compromise of sorts was reached in 1874. In that year Congress ratified the Brunot Agreement calling for the Utes to cede the mountaintops to the United States. This area amounted to one-quarter of the traditional Ute range, or some twelve million acres. The tribe retained lower lands to the south and west, which miners still had to cross to get to the shafts. Expectedly, confrontations and racial hatred mounted. Four years later Fort Lewis, no more than a few tents pitched along a raw dirt street, was placed at Pagosa Springs to keep the peace. It was on land claimed by the Capotes. Nonetheless, an atmosphere of cordiality reigned in a July 4th celebration at the springs, with tepees nudged against tents. With settlement expanding westward, in 1881 Fort Lewis was moved to the La Plata drainage.

From the time Colorado was declared a territory in 1861, there was loud agitation to rid the region of the Utes. Precious minerals and hidden valleys promising fertile fields were there for exploitation by immigrant whites, not Native Americans. Feeling that a relatively small tribe should not have exclusive use of such a boundless territory, the government set aside two Indian reservations within the state. This measure did not satisfy those who wanted the Utes out entirely. Matters came to a head after an agent at the White River agency and six of his staff were brutally murdered and the agent's wife and daughter were kidnapped by Utes in the so-called Meeker Massacre. An army unit precipitated the tragedy by marching into Indian land against treaty provisions. Regardless, all the northern Ute bands then were banished to a reservation in northeastern Utah. The Capotes and Moaches fared better. They were allowed to stay in Colorado on a Pine River reservation incorporating

728,320 acres of original Capote range. A few years later the Wimi-nuches chose to settle on a more westerly reservation.

The opening up of the San Juan mining district stimulated the movement of Hispanos out of the Tierra Amarilla–Chama area into the upper San Juan district. These newcomers were primarily teamsters plying a new toll road built from the New Mexican settlements down Canyon Largo on the west side of the Continental Divide to the San Juan River. A further influx of Hispanos came through the construction of the narrow gauge Denver, Rio Grande and Western Railroad, running from Antonito in the San Luis Valley over Cumbres Pass, then westward along the mesas falling away from the high mountains, to the San Juan River and eventually on to Durango. The tracks, laid across the Southern Ute Indian Reservation without official sanction, brought in another element: Hispanic sheepherders who could now get their animals from pasture to market. One prominent arrival was Antonio Archuleta, rancher and member of the young Colorado legislature, who proposed a county in the new area. It was established and named after him. A bit of northern New Mexico ambience was transplanted to another frontier when Hispanos built compounds of gable-roofed jacal or adobe structures recalling those in the Chama area, with a welter of outbuildings, grist mills, corn cribs, privies, and corrals. By 1880 there were at least eight tiny Hispanic communities trying to put down roots along the San Juan drainages. Once more the region evolved as an isolated refuge removed from the scenes of major action, a backwater where survival depended on the subsistence economy of orchards, kitchen gardens, root cellars, and sheep. Inbred and marginal in every sense, these Hispanos depended for solidarity upon familial and spiritual bonds that became more conservative and unchanging through time.

Meanwhile, because the Utes' hunting and gathering possibilities were being eliminated by the march of civilization, the U.S. government returned to the old idea of making farmers out of them. In 1886 a program to give Southern Utes land under a severalty arrangement was begun. A family could acquire an individual allotment of 160 acres. The prospects for the success of this plan were in doubt, not only because private ownership of land was foreign to the Ute way of thinking but also because farming remained anathema to them. By 1891 only thirty-five families

Hispanic family on the move from northern New Mexico to southern Colorado, probably in the late nineteenth century. *Courtesy Colorado Historical
Society.*

A Ute and his buggy in front of his teepee, with no farmland in sight. *Courtesy Center for Southwest Studies, Fort Lewis College.*

Ute house and brush *ramada* that may have been either copied after those of the early Hispanic settlers in the upper San Juan area or actually built by them. *Courtesy Center for Southwest Studies, Fort Lewis College.*

127

Hispanic Penitente rites taking place in the upper San Juan area. Men in foreground carry whips used for self-flagellation. *Courtesy Center for Southwest Studies, Fort Lewis College.*

had begun to farm. Others took some land but hired the newly arrived Hispanos to clear it, dig irrigation ditches, build houses, and raise crops on shares or leases. Lands the Utes did not use were considered surplus and were opened to whites. This furthered the Hispanic homestead style of life and led to a checkerboard pattern of non-Indian holdings within the reservation. Eventually, 523,079 acres allotted to the Utes were sold to others.

The Piedra Valley fell into the category of surplus lands. At its juncture with Nutria Creek, Rubio Gallegos built a one-room cabin of hand-hewn logs chinked with clay and farmed the bottomlands. Two Martínez families took homesteads near Stollsteimer Mesa. Juan Román Gurule staked out a plot on the central Piedra. Antonio María Abeyta moved to Yellowjacket, west of the pinnacles. These and other neighbors participated in Penitente affairs at a *morada* erected within sight of Chimney Rock and Companion Rock. Each month their womenfolk prepared a small Catholic chapel at the junction of the Piedra River and

Utes dipping sheep, probably at the Arboles vat. *Courtesy Colorado Historical Society.*

Nutria Creek for a Mass conducted by a priest who rode there in a buggy from Arboles, a railroad town with a large sheep-dipping vat used by all the herders in the region.

The federal government absorbed three unclaimed townships along the northern rim of the Ute reservation into its forest- and land-management holdings. Included was the Chimney Rock district. An ancient Native American community and possible shrine was to become an Anglo-American tourist attraction.

Immigrants other than Hispanos also moved into the region. Most notable among them was Christian Stollsteimer, a German who developed a large ranch on the Nutria. Later this stream was renamed Stollsteimer in his honor. The *La Plata Miner* in 1880 reported, "Mr. Stollsteimer is one of the most successful stock men in southwestern Colorado, and has immense herds of cattle and sheep which roam over the mesas and foothills to the west of the San Juan river." Stollsteimer soon allied himself with the Hispanos and Indians. His seven children married into Spanish-American families, and he himself served for a time as agent to the Southern Utes and Jicarilla Apaches. During this tenure, he sought to drive Anglos out of the area.

However, Anglos were not to be denied the right to move along the expanding frontier. In the late 1870s Eli Perkins and John Peterson settled near where the Baker bridge spanned the upper Piedra. Shortly they had Henry Freeman, J. R. Scott, and R. A. Howe as neighbors. There was an undercurrent of racial tension. Relations between Utes and Hispanos generally were friendly, occasionally leading to intermarriages, but clashes between Utes and Anglos were frequent. One Ute, who had taken the name of George Washington, claimed land to the east of Chimney Rock; he permitted Hispanic sheepherders to cross it freely but charged Anglos a fee. Settlers Scott and Howe retaliated by putting up signs in English warning Indians to stay off their property. Utes wandering through the valley could not have read the signs, nor would they have heeded them. To them, this was *their* place.

The Twin War Gods, enshrined in stone, looked down.

Selected References

Adams, E. Charles
  1975 Causes of Prehistoric Settlement Systems in the Lower Piedra District, Colorado. Ph.D. dissertation, University of Colorado, Boulder.

Bertram, Jack B., and Nancy S. Hammack
  1991 Half-Baked Ovens. Further Excavations at the Oven Site, LA4169, Navajo Reservoir. Paper presented at annual meeting of the Society for American Archaeology, New Orleans.

Buckles, William G.
  1968 Archaeology in Colorado Historic Tribes: Utes. *Southwestern Lore,* Vol. 34, No. 3, 53–67.

Carlson, Roy L.
  1964 Two Rosa Phase Pit Houses. *Southwestern Lore,* Vol. 29, No. 4, 69–76.

Dittert, A. E.
  1958 Preliminary Archaeological Investigations in the Navajo Project Area of Northwestern New Mexico. *Museum of New Mexico Papers in Anthropology,* No. 1, Santa Fe.

Dittert, A. E., J. J. Hester, and Frank W. Eddy
  1961 An Archaeological Survey of the Navajo Reservoir District, Northwestern New Mexico. *School of American Research and Museum of New Mexico Monograph,* No. 23, Santa Fe.

Dittert, A. E., Frank W. Eddy, and Beth L. Dickey
  1963 Evidences of Early Ceramic Phases in the Navajo Reservoir District. *El Palacio,* Vol. 70, 5–12.

Eddy, Frank W.
  1961 Excavations at Los Pinos Phase Sites in the Navajo Reservoir District. *Museum of New Mexico Papers in Anthropology,* No. 4, Santa Fe.
  1972 Culture Ecology and the Prehistory of the Navajo Reservoir District. *Southwestern Lore,* Vol. 38, Nos. 1–2, 1–75.
  1973 Pueblo Settlement Adaptations in the Upper San Juan Basin of New Mexico and Colorado, A.D. 1–1125. Paper presented at annual meeting of the Society for American Archaeology, San Francisco.
  1977 Archaeological Investigations at Chimney Rock Mesa: 1970–1972. *Memoirs of the Colorado Archaeological Society,* No. 1.

1990   Recent Archaeological Research at Chimney Rock Mesa, Southwestern Colorado. In *From Chimney Rock to Chaco,* papers of the Chimney Rock Archaeological Conference, Fort Lewis College, Durango. Forthcoming.

Ellis, Florence M.
1973   A Thousand Years of the Pueblo Sun-Moon-Star Calendar. Paper presented at annual meeting of the American Association for the Advancement of Science, Mexico City.
1988   *From Drought to Drought: Gallina Culture Patterns.* Vol 1. Sunstone Press, Santa Fe.

Ellis, Florence M. and J. J. Brody
1964   Ceramic Stratigraphy and Tribal History at Taos Pueblo. *American Antiquity,* Vol. 29, No. 3, 316–327.

Ford, Richard, Albert H. Schroeder, and Stewart L. Peckham
1972   Three Perspectives on Pueblo Prehistory. In *New Perspectives on the Pueblos.* Edited by Alfonso Ortiz. University of New Mexico Press, Albuquerque, 22–40.

Gilbert, Elizabeth X.
1961   A Pithouse Village on the San Juan River, New Mexico. *Southwestern Lore,* Vol. 27, No. 1, 9–16.

Hibben, Frank C.
1948   The Gallina Architectural Forms. *American Antiquity,* Vol. 14, No. 1, 32–36.
1949   The Pottery of the Gallina Complex. *American Antiquity,* Vol. 14, No. 3, 194–202.

Jeancon, Jean Allard
1922   *Archaeological Research in the Northeastern San Juan Basin of Colorado During the Summer of 1921.* Edited by Frank H. H. Roberts. State Historical and Natural History Society of Colorado and the University of Denver, Denver, 1–31.
1924   Archaeological and Ethnological Research During the Year of 1924. Unpublished manuscript at the Colorado Historical Society, Denver.
1925   Archaeological and Ethnological Research During the Year of 1925. Unpublished manuscript at the Colorado Historical Society, Denver.

Jeancon, Jean Allard, and Frank H. H. Roberts
1923   Archaeological Research in the Northeastern Basin of Colorado During the Summer of 1922. *Colorado Magazine,* Vol. 1, No. 1, 11–36; No. 2, 65–70; No. 3, 108–118; No. 4, 163–173; No. 5, 213–224; No. 6, 260–276; No. 7, 301–307.

Kane, Allen E.
1986   Organizational Models for Northern Chacoan Outlier Communities. Paper presented at the Third Anasazi Conference, Monument Valley, Arizona.

Lange, Charles H.
  1956   The Evans Site and the Archaeology of the Gallina Region, New Mexico. *El Palacio*, Vol. 63, No. 3, 72–90.

LeGare, David
  1990   Piedra/Gallina Analogs. In *From Chimney Rock to Chaco*, papers of the Chimney Rock Archaeological Conference, Fort Lewis College, Durango. Forthcoming.

Lister, Robert H., Stephen J. Hallisy, Margeret H. Kane, and George E. McLellan
  1970   Site 5LP11, a Pueblo I Site Near Ignacio, Colorado. *Southwestern Lore*, Vol. 35, No. 4, 57–67.

Malville, J. McKim, and Claudia Putnam
  1989   *Prehistoric Astronomy in the Southwest*. Johnson Books, Boulder.

Marsh, Charles S.
  1982   *People of the Shining Mountains*. Pruett Publishers, Boulder.

Marshall, Michael L., John R. Stein, Richard W. Loose, and Judith E. Novotny
  1979   *Anasazi Communities of the San Juan Basin*. Department of the Interior, Heritage Conservation and Recreation Service, Santa Fe.

Motter, John M.
  1984   *Pagosa Country: The First Fifty Years*. Privately printed, Pagosa Springs, Colorado.

Newren, Marcia T., Peter McKenna, and W. James Judge
  1990   The Place of Chimney Rock in the Chaco Network. In *From Chimney Rock to Chaco*, papers of the Chimney Rock Archaeological Conference, Fort Lewis College, Durango. Forthcoming.

Parsons, Elsie Clews
  1939   *Pueblo Indian Religion*. 2 vols. University of Chicago Press, Chicago.

Powers, Robert P., William B. Gillespie, and Stephen H. Lekson
  1983   *The Outlier Survey: A Regional View of Settlement in the San Juan Basin*. National Park Service, Division of Cultural Research, Albuquerque.

Prescott, William H.
  1844   *History of the Conquest of Mexico*. Random House, New York. Modern Library reprint.

Roberts, Frank H. H.
  1922   Report on the Work of the 1922 Season in the Piedra Parada Archaeological Field. *University of Denver Bulletin*, Vol. 23, No. 9.
  1925   Report on an Archaeological Reconnaissance in Southwestern Colorado in the Summer of 1923. *Colorado Magazine*, Vol. 2, No. 2, 3–84.
  1930   Early Pueblo Ruins in the Piedra District, Southwestern Colorado. *Bureau of American Ethnology Bulletin*, No. 96.

Schaafsma, Polly
  1963   Rock Art in the Navajo Reservoir District. *Museum of New Mexico Papers in Anthropology,* No. 7.

Schroeder, Albert H.
  1965   A Brief History of the Southern Utes. *Southwestern Lore,* Vol. 30, No. 4, 53–78.

Sullivan, Mary
  1990   Chimney Rock Ceramics. In *From Chimney Rock to Chaco,* papers of the Chimney Rock Archaeological Conference, Fort Lewis College, Durango. Forthcoming.
  1990b Clusters of Clay: A Compositional Analysis of Ceramics From Chimney Rock. M.A. thesis, University of Colorado, Boulder.

Swadesh, Frances Leon
  1966   Hispanic Americans of the Ute Frontier From the Chama Valley to the San Juan Basin, 1694–1960. Ph.D. dissertation, University of Colorado, Boulder.

Thompson, G. C.
  1972   Southern Ute Lands, 1848–1899. *Center for Southwest Studies Occasional Paper,* No. 1, Fort Lewis College, Durango.

Truell, Marcia
  1975   1972 Archaeological Explorations at the Ravine Site, Chimney Rock, Colorado. M.A. thesis, University of Colorado, Boulder.

Tucker, Gordon C.
  1981   The Prehistoric Settlement System on Chimney Rock Mesa, South-Central Colorado, A.D. 925–1125. Ph.D. dissertation, University of Colorado, Boulder.

Vivian, R. Gwinn
  1990   *The Chacoan Prehistory of the San Juan Basin.* Academic Press, New York.

INDEX